# DID I EXIST BEFORE? *and* WILL I BE BORN AGAIN?

A Quest into the Quest of all

**Suniti Chandra Mishra**

*Published by*

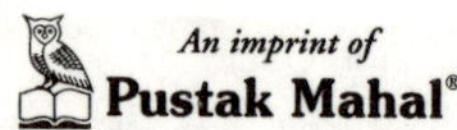


J-3/16 , Daryaganj, New Delhi-110002
☎ 23276539, 23272783, 23272784 • *Fax:* 011-23260518
*E-mail:* info@pustakmahal.com • *Website:* www.pustakmahal.com

***Sales Centre***

• 10-B, Netaji Subhash Marg, Daryaganj, New Delhi-110002
☎23268292, 23268293, 23279900 • *Fax:* 011-23280567
*E-mail:* rapidexdelhi@indiatimes.com

• **Hind Pustak Bhawan**
6686, Khari Baoli, Delhi-110006, ☎23944314, 23911979

***Branches***

**Bengaluru:** ☎ 080-22234025 • *Telefax:* 080-22240209
*E-mail*: pustak@airtelmail.in • pustak@sancharnet.in
**Mumbai:** ☎ 022-22010941 • 022-22053387
*E-mail*: rapidex@bom5.vsnl.net.in
**Patna:** ☎ 0612-3294193 • *Telefax:* 0612-2302719
*E-mail*: rapidexptn@rediffmail.com
**Hyderabad:** *Telefax:* 040-24737290
*E-mail*: pustakmahalhyd@yahoo.co.in



ISBN 978-81-223-1122-8

**Edition : 2010**



***Printed at :*** Param Offsetters, Okhla, Delhi

# Dedication

I dedicate this book
To my "friend forever"
Of vali-asr avenue,
Asad-abadi street,
Tehran (Iran)
Who 'inspired' me
For this work
And on whom
My soul has
Everlasting claims.

Tell me not in mournful numbers
Life is but an empty dream!
For the soul is dead that slumbers,
And things are not what they seem.

Life is real!  Life is earnest!
And the grave is not its goal;
Dust thou art, to dust returnest,
Was not spoken of the soul.

*- H.W. Longfello*

# Contents

# Preface

DID I EXIST BEFORE is a theosophical book dwelling on the subject of 'life before and after this mortal realm'. Based on his perceptions of the life principles, the author strives to establish that the creation is a process beyond any beginning or end in which each soul is 'separated' from the Great Soul for a spiritual 'Hide-and-Seek', to find Him back using his own free will.

To make this Hide-and-Seek intricate and interesting, God (The Great Soul) inspired each soul to find his or her soul-mate and rush together to meet Him. Those who found their soul-mates are close to finding God since 'human heart' is the common dwelling-place of both 'Beloveds'. Material love becomes a tunnel through which one emerges in the realm of Immortal Love.

The way to God is through this colourful, transient world. This finite world contains in itself both potentials for a soul – every atom guides here to the abode of the Most Beloved and, simultaneously, it has messes and snares to withhold the seeker from journeying to the Divine. Every soul is free to choose its course - either to behold this mortal charm from an 'eternal' vista or witness this eternal magic of life from a 'mortal' vista. To wander and be lost in this forest ... or drink its fresh-gushing water, partake of its yummy fruits, and – fresh and rejuvenated – rush to the Beloved.

With the sequential fluttering of the wings of 'free will' and 'destiny' the swan of the soul will soar to the sky – leaving the indelible trails of '*karma*' which will guide his journey further ... in the next life! This journey will continue till the Beloved is met!

Praise be unto each and all, known and unknown, who assisted me in completing this book. Everything in this universe is a vibration of consciousness. Everything is there to teach us some lesson. The 'Ishopanishada' says: "Ishàvàsyam idamsarvam yatkinchya jagatyàmjagat" (Whatever exists in this universe – animate or inanimate – is enveloped by the Divine).

Wherever a quotation is used in this book, efforts were made to seek permission from the copyright holders but it was not possible always and some short excerpts were taken as 'fair use' and mentioned in the footnotes. The book has used Baha'i quotations which are mostly taken from the official website of the Baha'i Faith – www.bahai.org – and other independent sources (mentioned in the contexts). I tried my best to use an authentic translation of the Geeta and the Quran, after seeking permission from the copyright-holders.

# Believe it or Leave it

> *Genius is experience. Some seem to think that it is a gift of talent, but it is the fruit of long experience in many lives. Some are older souls than others, and so they know more.*
>
> *— Henry Ford*

**Seeing with Coloured Glasses**

The greatest impediment to revelation of truth has ever been our 'coloured spectacles' to see it. We never stand near truth as an 'unknown', 'unlearned', 'unachieved', and 'unprejudiced' individual. The first thing we do before setting an 'appointment' with truth is to wear our spectacles, because we are always afraid thinking 'oh, what if the colour of truth is something else than I believe?' So, some go wearing Hindu specs, some put on Christian goggles, others have Islamic binoculars .... and there are many other spectacles! An average Hindu stands there defensive of his deep-rooted belief in 'reincarnation'. A Muslim is fully alert that no fact should appear that proves the theory of reincarnation because, as they say, it is against the teaching of Islam. A Christian also stands quite ready with his protective radars 'ON', so that nothing goes against Christian teachings that have no belief in rebirth. Similarly, a Baha'i has his own defensive shield, because their religion does not believe in 'reincarnation' in line with the Hindu concepts, and a Buddhist appears with a different posture. Nothing can be worse treatment of truth than seeing it with eyes fully blind and mind completely unreceptive.

I feel that everyone who is going to read this book should, for a moment, hurl away his or her 'isms' in the Indian Ocean (or the Pacific Ocean, if that is nearer!) Please don't tailor the truth according to your tenet but tailor your tenet according to the truth.

I personally have a great respect for all religions and their teachings and I am a person whose daily prayer session includes sincere reading of verses from the Geetā, the Quran, the Bible and Baha'i Prayers, and, if I can get, I would like to add more Scriptures. That's because I want to see the truth from several windows so that my mind settles in complete certitude. At the same time, I also maintain that each individual has to find his or her truth by himself or herself, because truth is a very 'relative' term ..... relative with time, with space, with individual, with the level of knowledge which is always in progressive mode, etc. and yet truth is 'absolute', too! These two aspects of 'truth' – its relativity and absoluteness – must be observed carefully to grasp the full picture. What Krishna said in his time was not all contextual with a progressive time. For example, he said that he created four 'varnas' (professionals, castes or groups based on their work and skills): Brahmins, the learned class; Kshatriyas, the ruler and warrior class; Vaishyas, the trader class; and Shudras, the serving class. *The Geetā, 4 : 13.*

*Chāturvarnyam mayā srishtam guna karma vishāgashah;*
*Tasya kartāram api mām vidvaya kartāram avyayam.*

Can even a staunch Hindu honestly admit today that this 'classification' is just and applicable in today's society? Is it possible to divide this complex human society, with ever-increasing activities day by day, in these four 'compartments', especially when they became a class-order based on exalting one over the other? The fact is: many things that Krishna taught and many things that he did not specifically teach were 'relative' to his time, relative to the capacity and receptivity of the people of his time. There are many things that Krishna did not 'talk about' at all. For example, he did not reveal any significant amount of teaching about "equality of men and women" but **Baha'u'llah** did so. While reading the Scriptures, we must remember this specific nature of truth. Now, since Krishna did not say anything about equality of men and women, it does not mean that he did not consider this equality valid or he was against the equality of men and women. In his indirect teachings and through his personal example he amply showed that he loved and safeguarded women and valued their dignity.

The story of Draupadi whom He helped when she was being humiliated in the court of Duryodhana is an important example.

## Limitations of Scriptures

Every religion in its respective time teaches the 'core values' relevant for that time. Every Messenger appears as a divine Teacher who teaches us on two bases – first, the 'spiritual curriculum' prescribed by God and, second, the receptivity of the people. Just consider yourself to be a pupil in Grade 1. The teacher who came to teach you is learned enough to guide you into the principles of syntax and etymology, but he limits himself to teaching you alphabet and simple words. Because the syllabus prescribed to him does not allow him to go beyond that nor it will be in your capacity to know about etymology and syntax before you have learnt alphabet.

Geetā, Zendavesta, Tattvarthasutra, Tripitak, Bible, Talmud, Analects, Kojiki, Chuang-tzu, Quran, Bayan, Aqdas, Adi Granth – whatever Scripture can be named, none of them deal with "each and all" spheres of human life, they do not shed guidance on A to Z matters of spiritual realm. We cannot therefore make any Scripture a final basis to prove or dis-prove everything. They all focus on the 'most vital teaching for that time' and other matters become secondary. For example, the main emphasis of the Bible is on God's kindness and the sins of the human beings and the appearance of the Christ to save them from sins by offering his own life. Christianity is the religion of "faith" and "forgiveness" and the "immensity of God's kindness" that culminated in the sacrifice of His own chosen son – Jesus Christ. The Quran focuses on the orders and disciplines of human life and the ultimate peace and salvation of mankind in surrendering before Allah. It deals with several other topics, as does Bible, but the main focus is on these things only. Baha'u'llah lays his emphasis on practical activities with spiritual intents that can advance the human civilisation as a unified body. Though his writings shed light on many mystical aspects, his exhortation to mankind is to refrain from idle imaginings and waste no time in the pursuit of such knowledge that 'begins with word and ends with word'. Lord Krishna had appeared in a different time when the subjects dealt in the Bible or the Quran or the Aqdas were not so relevant but the knowledge about the nature of soul was to be imparted essentially to an innocent-hearted seeker whose name was Arjuna (literally meaning, 'the simple one'). Let's always remember this time-specific truth of the Holy Books and the Messengers of God before concluding anything.

**Rebirth in Christianity and Islam**

Do Christianity and Islam believe in rebirth? This becomes a weighty question only when we first ask: Have Christianity and Islam dealt specifically with this question in any dedicated chapter or explanatory passage of the Bible and the Quran respectively? As stated above, these Scriptures had to focus on other aspects of life and spiritualism according to the mandate of God, but the "Geetā" deals with it in length, especially in its 2nd and 6th Chapters. However, many passages in the Bible and the Quran clearly refer to concepts like "rebirth", "life again", "heaven" and "a world beyond this world" and such things, in the same way as "Geeta" also teaches about the power of faith and surrender to God as an 'under-current'.

Is there no belief in the previous life expressed in the **Old Testament** or the **New Testament**? Is it not true that Jesus Christ referred to the arrival of Prophet Elijah as John the Baptist?

> *"But I say to you that Elijah has come already, and they did not know him but did to him whatever they wished. Likewise the Son of Man is also about to suffer at their hands". .... Then the disciples understood that He spoke to them of John the Baptist.*
>
> (The Bible, Matthew 17: 12,13)

What is the meaning of the Resurrection of the Christ?

The day of life and the night of death have kept on recurring from the time immemorial and so will it be till the end that has no end.

> *It is You who causes the night to slip into the day and the day to slip into the night. You bring forth the alive from the dead and the dead from the alive. You give provision to whomsoever You want... .*
>
> (The Quran, III:27)

What does it mean that there is a 'Day of Judgment' when each being will be 'raised up again' and brought before Allah for reckoning? You are given a 'second birth' (raised up again) .... that is also rebirth. And within a 'second birth', who knows, you have a lifespan of 'several births'! I gave you $5000 in one payment or in several instalments, it is almost the same thing. We live only one life after this life for 5000000000000000 years or live several lives in this span of time, what's the difference? These 5000000000000000 years will not remain the same always, different experiences will keep us changing and that is like 'taking many births' or we can be born many, many times in that infinite span! What's the difference? It is said that when a foetus is in the embryo, its frame and features change every few seconds. By the time it is out in this world, it has taken 'several births' though we consider it a single birth. In the Quran, there is a passage which goes like this:

> *He who was passing by a ruined settlement and who exclaimed: Will Allah enliven this settlement after its decay? Then Allah made him die for a hundred years and revived him again. He asked as to how long did he tarry, and (the man ) replied: 'a day or a part thereof'. Allah said: 'You tarried for a hundred years. Look at your spoiled food and drink, and your ass. Look at the bones so that we make you a token unto mankind, and see how we join everything and cover with flesh'. When everything was thus evident, he said: Allah is surely able to do everything.*
>
> (The Quran 2:259)

Throughout these Holy Texts and elsewhere, in a general sense, the term 'man' also refers to 'woman' *mutatis mutandis*.

This passage has three important messages: 1. Allah can re-shape a thing after its death or destruction, 2. Allah is beyond time and space, and 3. Allah is able to do all things. Thus, what we calculate as 'one', 'two', and 'three' or as 'first', 'second' and 'third' will be quite insignificant for the Supreme. *Even in our one lifetime in this birth, we take new birth several times. Not only our cells but even our mental dispositions completely change. We rise to a new level of consciousness almost every day. Thus, the same eternal soul enters into a 'new body' each time we grow into a teen from a child, into an adult person from a teen, and into an old being from an adult. In this sequence, death is only a next stage of life after oldness.*

It is hurting to know that in many Islamic countries, incidents related to the memories of previous birth are intentionally suppressed because they think it goes against Islam. It equally hurts to know that many people in India forcefully relate the syndromes of a mental disease to the reminiscences of one's previous birth. The hesitations of Islam as well as Baha'i Faith are basically due to their belief that **'Nobody can be a partner with God'**. They fear that by accepting that an individual soul existed before, they will proclaim its partnership with God. In the same way, the fear of Christianity in accepting reincarnation is that reincarnation believes in gradual evolution of soul, from primal to advanced stages of awareness culminating in 'nirvāna' or salvation; whereas Christianity has already concluded that all humans are sinners and no human being can ever achieve that perfect state of a pure soul.

**No Individual Soul: No Partnership**

Neither Islam nor Christianity needs to fear, because the truth that every soul existed before in the Great Soul and will eventually blend in the Great Soul has nothing to do with 'partnership' with God nor does it argue that one day a soul can be Pure like God. When we dip a million vessels in the sea, each vessel receives a 'part of the sea' and yet no vessel is a 'partner of the sea'. The image of the sun can reflect in a thousand mirrors but no mirror can claim to be a 'partner' of the sun. The 'sea' contained in the vessel was already in the Sea. The light reflecting in a mirror always belongs to the sun in its originality. The Geetā tells us that soul is not something that 'comes' or 'exits', 'enters' or 'leaves'. It is free from birth and death:

*Na Jāyate mriyate wā Kadāchinnāyam*
*bhutvā bharitā wā bhyyah;*
*Ajo nityah shāshvato ayam purāro*
*na hanyate hanyamāne sharire.*

*This soul is not born in any time nor does it meet death. It is not something that happens (or becomes) or ceases to happen. This soul is free from birth. It is perpetual, eternal, and timeless. It does not die by the death of the body.*

(The Geetā, 2 : 20)

Bodies come and exit, enter and leave. Exactly, as in the case of the mirror and the sun, there is no light in the mirror itself but the light of the sun appears in it.

What we know as individual souls of John and Christina, Ramesh and Nina, Saleem and Zena are not, in truth, 'individual souls' in the same way as no mirror actually contains any 'individual' light. When 'bodies' appear in any form, the Light of the Truth is shed on them and we see different reflections in different mirrors. This is only a phantasmagoria, a meaningful phantasmagoria created by God for a purpose – and the purpose is the soul's realisation of love for God. Thus, in actual sense, there is only one SOUL reflecting in all and there is no question of 'partnership with God' when 'partners' do not even 'exist'.

In the same way, no soul can ever attain that level of purity which can be acceptable in the holy presence of God. I remember, when I was a middle school student, children of my grade were encouraged to adopt Sanskrit as an 'optional language'. The teachers used to say that those who will opt Sanskrit will get high scores. Really! Students who chose other vernaculars were getting hardly 60-70% while we, who chose Sanskrit, were scoring beyond 80%. All this 'encouragement' was because Sanskrit was becoming an obsolete language by that time and its revival was necessary. In a time when love for God and likeness for being good and noble is becoming outdated, a 'pure' soul means even a soul that at least prays sincerely or fulfils some other minimal requirements is required. This grade of 'purity' has nothing to do with soul's deservingness. God wants to 'encourage' this purity in the same way as my teachers wanted to promote Sanskrit as a noble language. No doubt, we all are sinners and that's why the Saviour came to absolve us. It does not mean, however, that we should not try to be 'pure'. God is the embodiment of justice, but if He is to deal with us with His iron rule of justice, each one of us would be doomed to hell. But He prefers to deal with us with kindness and He counts even a little good act on our part as a point of promotion of our soul. A little effort of the soul towards virtue is immensely praiseworthy in the divine realm where kindness rules more than strictness:

> *When Allah decreed the Creation, He pledged Himself by writing in His book which is laid down with Him: My mercy prevails over my wrath.*
>
> (Hadith, Qudsi 1)

Truth cannot surface until we throw out our coloured spectacles and get free from the barriers of religious fears and prejudices. There is no need to fear that if we unmoor our boats and sail across the ocean of truth, boldly and adventurously, it will offend Mohammad or displease the Christ, infuriate Baha'u'llah or disgrace Krishna. God Himself is Truth and these Messengers came to show us that Truth only. We really don't need such Messengers and even God if they revenge upon us for a pure, intent voyage to the shore of truth, but no, we are ourselves afraid and indecisive. How assuring it is to know that truth is unchangeable and all Messengers came from the same Source! It is NOT POSSIBLE that Krishna said something which **Mohammad** confronted and what Jesus Christ said about the absolute truth was in contradiction with the teachings of Baha'u'llah. But it is POSSIBLE that we might have failed in correlating their basic teachings and in understanding them in their total relativity.

**Life: Unique and Individual**

Each individual here has a unique life – totally incomparable to the other. Each one seems to be carrying a unique mission, a unique thought pattern, a unique set of actions and reactions. Why does this uniqueness exist? Why all are not the same? And what factors decide each one's uniqueness? I have observed my own life and the lives of others. There are people who are born with perfections and a magic wand in their hand! And there are people who spend their life wiping the sweat of their brows and finding a petty nickel. We erroneously claim that those who succeed have bought success by paying its cost. Many, many have paid these costs and yet success seems far from them. Many have followed these 'rules of wealth and success' but the result was not so great! The others really 'came, saw and conquered'!

There are times when everything goes so easily. You receive the love of your life as easily as a powerful magnet attracts a piece of iron nearby. You become the 'apple of eye' of all the people around you. Everything goes as favourably as it is your natural right to get every good of the world. Money flows in your pocket as flowers bloom in spring. You bask in the sun of fame and glory; enjoy praise and approval coming from all sides. Whatever you touch becomes gold. And then, suddenly, the spring turns into autumn. The fondest love of your life is gone and won't come back even if you scream and lament so deplorably. All the wealth of life evaporates: wealth not only in the terms of 'money' but also in the terms of peace and wellness, charm and glory. All the flowers fade away and only thorns are there to rule. All lights have disappeared and you are enveloped in an abysmal darkness. Even if you touch something with a magic wand, no change is there, oh! No effect. According to a Japanese proverb: ***"When the unlucky man begins to sell coffins, people stop dying"***.

And then again the wheel turns. While you are sleeping hopelessly in your night of dearth, a warbling sound awakens you. A bird chirps and you open the window and, lo! The dried-up river of life starts warbling again. The bird of hope is chirping. There is sunlight, there is music. A new love dawns in your life, a new glory is smiling on you with a dazzling crown in her hands. You get a 'new life'! Who says 'life' is only after 'death'? Even in this same physical existence I died many times and many times I was reborn. I am the same but not the same today. There is something in me that is intact but still I am completely changed. 'Death', as we call and know it, only marks my 'visible disappearance' from a manifest state but who knows even that is 'Life', though not visible to our earthly eyes! Many times I 'disappeared' even when you felt you are seeing me, feeling my presence, but you never knew I have 'come again', a completely new being .... and you know not!

I know, for those who do not want to believe in 'reincarnation', it is easy to say that this is a natural pattern of life, that whatever happened to me were just consequences. But why? Why is it so that we live in the same world, sharing the same resources of nature, basking under the same sunlight, living the same life as everyone else does, subjected to the same universal laws, and yet each one of us is carrying a 'different world' around him or her? Why these ups and downs of life come as my individual fate? Why don't all have the same destiny? If God is Just, as we call Him, why there are so many differences and discriminations? What is the meaning of my individual life and why so?

These and many other questions have recently made me utterly dismayed and engrossed in finding a satisfactory answer. This book is not written to prove the belief in 'rebirth' nor is it written to disprove it. Many close experiences of my life prompted me to write this book based on my own perception and I just responded to this inspiration; realising it well that I am not at all an authority on this matter. But it is good I am not an authority and so I have no 'spectacles'. I will have no hesitation to admit, if it is strongly brought to my realisation, that my belief in the previous birth and life after death might have been a mistaken belief. I have nothing to defend but my own soul and sincerity. I am here with my eyes open, ears alert, mind free, to investigate into a query that I faced so vehemently. I also know that this universe is like a mirror that reflects our own faith. Those who "don't want" to believe in this theory or anything, will "never believe" and those who "want to believe" because of their individual needs and tendencies will "always find something" to keep up their belief. This book is a humble tribute to both of them. As **Martin Luther King** said, ***"Every man must do two things alone - his own believing and his own dying."*** I leave it on you: Believe it or leave it!

**

## 2

# The Stage is Set

> *Neither knowledge nor hope for the future can be the pivot of our life or determine its direction. It is intended to be solely determined by allowing ourselves to be gripped by the ethical God, who reveals Himself in us, and by our yielding our will to His.*
>
> *— Albert Schweitzer*

The stage is set. The actors are ready. Cameramen are posed on their angles. Lights are on. My friend, Director Andrei Leonovich, is always busy shooting his legendary films that carve a niche in cine history. He is up and doing, shouting, consoling, encouraging, scolding, remaking, editing, admiring and sitting with me at the coffee table when everything is ok.

And then, one day, he invites me to the trailer of the film. It's a wonderful film, as always! The actors are great, the story is thrilling. Holding my breath, I watch scene after scene, curious to know what's going to happen next. But, for Andrei, he is cool and calm, sipping his coffee and watching the film all relaxed. I know he has worked diligently. He has been with the characters already, improved them, guided them and he knows what each of them is going to do. He has been working so assiduously with the writers and editors, light boys and cameramen that he knows every turn of the story with its focus, smell, colour, purport, and details!

With the last sip of the coffee, the trailer ended. I stood up, shook Andrei's hands warmly and said with a note of pride: "Congrats, Andrei! For your great, matchless acting!"

"Acting? Me?" He looked into my eyes curiously but I smiled back and walked towards my car.

Andrei Leonovich, though a film director by profession, is but one of the trillions of 'actors' performing their respective roles on this panoramic stage - the world!

The stage is set. The actors are ready. The only difference is that the Great Director has given each 'actor' the freedom to write his or her own story and perform his or her role in the best-suited manner according to his or her conscience, knowledge and intuition. This Great Director does not shout like Andrei, He edits nothing and lets the film develop as the actor wants it to develop. In fact, He does not interfere at all, except in sporadic instances when His interference will, in His surefire wisdom, alter the things in the fashion He designed. Of course, He encourages the actors and sends intuitive guidance for those who care to watch His signs in each atom of the universe.

And the most marvellous thing which makes the Great Director far ahead of the Andrei Leonovichs is this: though each actor is making his or her own story, He knows everything beforehand, even before the story is conceived!

> *It is He who holds the keys of the unseen. Only He knows them. And He knows what is on the land and in the sea. Even a leaf does not fall without His knowledge.... .*
>
> (The Quran, VI : 59)

> *So, arise! achieve renown, overcome the enemies and enjoy a lavish kingdom. All these warriors are already destroyed by me. O Savyasachi (Arjuna)! You just have to be an instrument (in my hands).*
>
> (Geetā, 11:33)

*Tasmātva utishtha yasho labhasva*
*jitvā shatrun bhungakshva rājyam smriddham;*
*Majaivaite nihatāh purvameva*
*nimittamātram bhava savyasāchin.*

In the 26th verse of the 7th chapter of Geeta, Krishna has already told Arjuna that ***He is well aware of everything and everyone that existed before, exists now and will exist in the future but He is not known by any.*** *Bhavishyāni cha bhutāni mām tu veda.* Thus, as actors of this ongoing, everlasting cosmic drama, our individual roles are already written in the thought of the One Who is the Initiator of all 'thoughts' and wellspring of all 'desires'. As we all exist in a Super Conscious Mind, there's no way to think and act above and beyond that reality. A fish cannot swim out of water, a flame cannot rise out off the fire, and the sun cannot outstrip the bounds of the sky.

**Apparently Mysterious**

Whatever we think and do – not only in THIS life but even in the life that we LIVED and WILL LIVE is already in the mind of the minds, but we don't know what things are kept hidden from us as mysteries. We don't know what blessings and curses it holds tomorrow, what joy and sorrow await us the moment hence. There is a divine wisdom in holding these as mysteries from us till they are actually revealed in due course in this journey of our soul.

Everything is kept intentionally hidden from us since Divine Wisdom wants us to become active agents in the process of life. When we think that it is 'we' who are doing everything, we assume conscious responsibility for our life and it is truly essential for the development of our soul. By assuming the direct role in this ongoing creative process, we receive the right of "free will" that can even alter our bad destiny tomorrow because the Super Conscious Mind is ever willing to change everything the moment we are willing to change our universe. Thus, as Tolstoy believed, we all are just playing our respective roles already written in our destiny, yet, since we don't know what is next on the 'script', we have no option than to think we are ourselves doing it!

> *Man lives consciously for himself, but is an unconscious instrument in the attainment of the historic, universal, aims of humanity.*
>
> (Leo Tolstoy)

**Destiny and Free-will**

There's a fine difference between destiny and free will which keeps people baffling throughout the life. This puzzle leaves their mind split up into two frames: Am I a puppet in a pre-ordained play or a chooser of my own role, a fashioner of my own fate? It becomes important for our mind to come to a conclusion regarding our true identity on this 'stage' of life that's set for us. **Albert Einstein** said: ***"There are only two ways to live your life. One is as though nothing is a miracle. The other is as though everything is a miracle"***, and we surely need to know which one is the right way!

Many problems are solved when we go into their 'roots'. The 'nearest past' I can trace about my existence is when I was in my mother's womb, yet to be born in this world! There in that darksome, squelchy membrane, I was an entity 'unknown' even to myself, till God bestowed upon me 'consciousness'. I had no independent choice. I breathed when my mother breathed. I ate what my mother ate, drank what my mother drank, dreamt what my mother dreamt, and thought what my mother thought. I had no destiny other than what my mother had. But as I was privileged with 'consciousness', I gradually began 'thinking of my own entity', and as I thought so, my entity was born. This 'thought' produced 'feelings', feelings produced 'desires', desires produced 'urges' and my urges prompted me to explore a larger world to which I belonged. I wriggled with an inexorable thrust to come out of my shell! And I was born! This was my second birth: the birth of an 'I', an 'ego', the birth of a 'conscious reality'. In the same way, we all exist in the large Embryonic World of the '*Brahma*', 'the 'Creator'.

> *My Primal Nature in the form of the Great Brahma is the womb of all the beings in which I implant the embryo of consciousness of all. Every being is shaped out of this association of the animate and the inanimate. ...From all the various wombs the 'images' (bodies) that come forth, Nature is the mother who conceives them all and I am the Father Who fertilises them.*
>
> (Geetā, 14: 3-4.)

*Mama yonih mahadbrahma tasmin garbham dadhāmyaham;*
*Sambhavah sarva bhutānām tato bhavati bhārata.*
*Sarvayonishu kaunteya murtayah sambhavanti yāh;*
*Tāsām brahma mahadyanih aham beeja pradah pitā.*

We exist in this cosmic shell as an entity hitherto unknown; depending for everything on the Mother Nature. We have no action of our own, no thought of our own, no consequence of our own. But the moment we are 'born' in this great embryo, consciousness is bestowed on us. This consciousness is my (our) individual property endowed by the Super Conscious. And out of this consciousness, my (our) individual reality sprang up, my individual feelings, individual desires crept out; my consciousness assumed the attributes of the Super Consciousness and longed to express itself in the same way as that Super Consciousness had desired to express itself by creating me and this entire cosmos. The same consciousness gave me the right to write my own destiny. The moment I strongly desired that 'may it so happen', the Author made the necessary modifications in my destiny and said 'so it be!'

Thus, destiny and free will are not far away from each other, neither at dagger's end, nor in isolated waters! ***'Everything is destined'*** means God has a definite plan for everything and everyone (and, no doubt, God's plan is victorious over everything), and ***'we have free will'*** means God's plans are flexible enough to give my valid desires and evolving consciousness their ample room. This mutual friendship between destiny and free will makes it sure that we are not living in a narrow world, in a rigid world, in a fixed realm, in a world so stingy that once 'written', nothing can change. Nay, we are living in a lavish world of a rich Father, in a world of countless possibilities, immense probabilities and plentiful opportunities!

It is well clarified by Krishna at the end of the Geetā 18:63. **In this way I have given you the most secret knowledge. After thinking well on all the aspects of this mysterious knowledge then do whatever you wish to do.** (The teachings of Krishna is the destiny, whatever Arjun will do is 'free-will'.)

*Iti te gyānam ākhyātam guhyād guhyataram mayā;*
*Wimrishya yetad sheshena yath ikshasi tathā kuru.*

The 'Law of Destiny' is one of the most mysterious laws of God. People always tend to hold one 'extreme' or the other, but perhaps it can be explained with the help of the following letters:

**N T G U S I H L**

These haphazard letters contain the probability of being made into several words, such as Sun, Sunlight, Light, Sunil, This, Hilt, Hunt, Night, Hit and so on. Originally, the letters are only 8 but they can be arranged in full or partial sequences to create a number of words. All these 'probabilities' are 'destined forms' of the letters N T G U S I H L. If they are arranged into 'Sun', it is that particular destiny but they could also be arranged into 'Light'. Even that could be their destiny. However, in all destinies, the properties (letters) are the same. John has some basic traits – wisdom, intelligence, presence of mind, logical thinking, imagination, physical strength, and courage. He has inherited these 'combinations' from his previous life actions. Now, with these combinations, he will always be challenged to choose a course of his life. He can use these capacities – through training and education, environmental help and support, self-decisions and counselling or whatever – to adopt a career as a 'detective', or a 'police officer', or a 'noted criminal', or a 'sports coach' or like things. All these are 'destinies' or 'probabilities' hidden in John. Thus, though he cannot go beyond the destined domains of his pre-earned skills, he can use his free will to determine the next direction of his skills. Each one of us has a number of probable destinies, if we just decide and change!

We are actors with our self-written roles: roles that we have been writing since ages and roles that we can always edit. Unfortunately, we often don't understand and accept that even now whatever we are thinking and doing, is leaving a 'trail' for our soul – a smell it will follow! Believing in destiny gives us a more profound sense of responsibility in making our life, because we will 'live' what we will 'make'. Perhaps many of us already know this story:

**Sun/Nit**

*There was a carpenter who worked with a rich and noble master. He used to make many 'items' for him. Then the carpenter became old and had to retire. The master called him and said, "Now that you are leaving, I wish you do a last favour to me".*

*"What?" The carpenter asked as he was afraid that even till the end of his workday, the 'cruel' master was not going to spare him.*

*The master said, "Just make a lovely wooden house. I have to gift it to someone very special".*

*The reluctant carpenter spent many months after that, somehow dragging himself to complete the work and go and retire. He did not care details. He did not invest the best of his arts. He could make a very nice, comfortable, beautiful and abiding house, but, alas!*

*He did not do so. When the work was finished and the house was made, the master came to him and giving him a golden key said: "I wanted to gift this house to you, my great carpenter! You served me with such dedication!"*

Alas! It is too late, on the verge of death, when we realise the generosity of our benevolent Master, our God. If we knew that this ephemeral 'wooden house of soul' – this life - is truly His gift to us, we could invest more time and art, more attention and devotion in 'making' it into the Garden of Eden. We could choose the most abiding canes and woods of eternal values; we could decorate it with fragrant arbours of love's jasmines and affection's daffodils; we could prepare the gardens of inner delight than brocades of 'come-and-go' merriments; and we could indent every great imagination to furnish its embellishments!

❋❋

## 3

# The Indomitable Force of Life

> My candle burns at both its ends;
> It will not last the night;
> But ah, my foes, and oh, my friends,
> It gives a lovely light.
>
> — *Edna St. Vincent Millay*

*Once, a poor young man met* ***H.G. Wells****, a famous writer, in his desire to get some financial help from him. The man was blind, lame, and looked completely desperate. He told H.G. Wells that life was a burden for him and he had no means to support himself. H.G. Wells replied: "Well, I can give you $500 for your eyes if you can donate them to me now. After all, they are both useless for you".*

*But the young man felt offended and said "What's this you say? I came seeking your favour". The writer then asked him to cut off one of his hands for him and he could offer him $5000. Since the young man was more infuriated now, he calmed him down: "Ok, no problem. I think you want to strike a good bargain. Will it be ok if I offer you $50000 and you give me your tongue?"*

*It was too much and the young man stood up and wanted to leave in his utmost fury. H.G. Wells smiled and said: "It means you have something more valuable than $50000!"*

**Life: A Gift, not a Burden**

Yes, even a 'seemingly useless' life is worth above $50000. And life is never a burden. If it is, throw it down if you can! Are you ready to die; now; at this very moment; ok, tomorrow, or the day after tomorrow? Even when we are in the most dismal state of our life, even when everything is lost, life is our love-point. We don't want to lose life. Life is precious.

Maharshi Vyas, the author of the epic "*Mahābhārata*", was once on his way. A chariot was coming from the opposite side. The seer poet saw a small insect creeping fast towards the bushes. Suddenly he laughed aloud and said to himself: "See this tiny insect! Its life is almost non-existent and yet when it heard the noise of the chariot, it escaped to save its worthless life from being crushed under the wheels".

Even a tiny insect loves its life. Death is no passion for any creature of God. Even if you are going to surely die the very next moment, you won't believe in death, you won't give up and leave the hope of life.

That is because life is generated from Life ... and not from death. Everything craves for what it is born from. Everything returns to its origin. If you throw a lump of soil in the sky, no matter howsoever powerfully you throw, it will come back to earth, because it is made up of the earth element. Vapour goes to the sky; it will never turn towards the earth, because its root is in hydrogen. If you burn a candle, its flame does not listen to the law of the earth's gravity; the flame is always upwards because its root is in fire that exists in the ether. Since we are created by God, Who is life Himself, it is natural for us to crave for life. Life will never like to meet death, it will never crave for death, and it will never dissolve in death, because its journey did not start from death. Life is real, death is false. 'Life is earnest and death is not its goal'.

**Lost Civilisations**

Death has been threatening life since time immemorial. Countless splendorous civilisations appeared and vanished. Perhaps we think that we are enjoying the highest level of culture and civilisation today, but human history says that many advanced cultures flourished on this earth before us. They were no less skilled in arts and sciences than we are today. Yet there is no trace of many of these civilisations now or they are thriving in an overlooked corner of the world with deteriorating charm. Where are now the glories of the Maya civilisation which flourished so well some 20000 years ago and where are their wonderful architecture, palaces, observatories, their astounding progresses in sciences, arts and engineering? Historians assume that the meltdown of glaciers drowned their existence. Even if they scarcely exist today, that richness of the past is gone. Where is today that prosperous Sumerian civilisation alongside the Euphrates River? Where's even a single trace of their rich culture based on agriculture and trade? Where are their mighty armies, their chariots and phalanxes? It is over 2500 years that their existence was deleted forever. Where is the pomp and glory of the Babylonian Empire? Where are those 'Suleymans' and those proud rulers of Ottoman Empire? Nor does today remain any trace of the great and systematic Indus-valley civilisation that thrived centuries ago in Harappa and Mohenjodaro. A deadly flood came and swept away their power or a famine or epidemic killed their people. And where is that invincible Byzantine Empire of Europe with Constantinople as its centre of spellbinding charm? Theodosius-II made a strong impregnable wall to protect his city from attacks, but death still intruded. Justinians' valour could not safeguard this great empire of a time nor are there any precious remains acquired in the Gothic Wars. Their jewelled clothes and embroidered costumes are lost forever.

Death came and snatched the glory of Roman Empire. Death came and usurped the power of Persian rulers. Assyrians, Cimmerians, Hittites, Lydians, Minoans, Nubians, Phoenicians, Scythians and many, many other ancient civilisations were blown by death in a matter of minute. And they were all so majestic civilisations: with the most beautiful women we could ever imagine, the most talented people we could think of, profuse wealth and power beggaring description, and advancement of such level which leaves us bewildered! They all ended. So what? Did life cease to be? No more charming women were born? No wonderful talents were created? No more poets, artists and scientists came? Did advancement come to a standstill? No more marvellous structures were built? No more melodious songs were sung? Death blew its hammer heavy and hard. Life got a fatal jolt. It squirmed in pain. It screamed and sobbed. It was plundered and robbed. But it smiled again. Oh! a very sweet smile that defies death, the cruel!

And then there are numerous natural calamities like floods, cyclones, tsunamis, earthquakes, volcanic eruptions and so on. Even if we take into account just the data of last century, and consider only one continent – Asia, more than 30000000 people died in major disasters like Great Indian Famine in 1876, China Floods in 1887 and 1931, Bangladesh Cyclone in 1970, Iran Blizzard in 1972, Indian Ocean Tsunami in 2004 – just to mention a few! In bygone days, many more deadly catastrophes were faced by humanity, such as Black Death in Europe which swept over a horrendous 100,000,000 lives in the year 1348. Earthquakes and volcanic eruptions in last few centuries deleted the trace of over 5 million human lives from the surface of earth. These threats are not new. Many islands and settlements were erased to dust in remote past by the outburst of lava. In 1883, the volcanic eruption on Krakatoa killed over 35000 people in just one blow. Death came disguised in many ways: as storms and tornadoes, landslides and wildfires, diseases and famines, wrecks and rampages. From time to time, the earth has also been attacked by astral entities. In 1908, an asteroid hit Siberia 'killing' some 80 million trees. Had it fallen over a populated area, just imagine!

And as if nature's wrath was not enough, a handful of blind and bigot 'wolves in human forms' waged wars to feed even larger crumbs to death. Human history is 'aglow' with the details of wars in a very 'glorified' manner as if wars proved a very high status of mankind. Being a knight, a hero, a warrior, a killer has always been credited more importance than being a poet, a writer, a humanitarian, a philosopher, an artist, a spiritual soul. Hundreds of battles have been fought since emergence of this earth. Only the last two World Wars have massacred millions of people.

Did life stop? Is Hiroshima sobbing still? Nay, it has bloomed into a far beautiful city. Have you visited a place where flood or earthquake, cyclone or storms played havoc just a few years ago? Go, and you will see life smiling there, houses rebuilt, roads reconstructed, resources rearranged, withered faces beaming with life again. Volcanoes might have been very powerful but not stronger than the soul's desire to live, to relive, relive and relive.

Life has always been stronger than death because life is "element" of God. Death is "element" of Nature. The body dies when it becomes too old and incapable of fulfilling the missions of the soul. What is the mission of the soul? Example of a candle and its flame has been given above. The flame belongs to fire; therefore it aspires to go upward to the ether to meet its originator, the fire. But the candle is made up of wax, and wax is earthen. Everything returns to its source. This body made up of earth returns to earth. This soul made up of Light, goes to Light. The river dissolves in the ocean. EVERYTHING RETURNS TO ITS ROOT .... sooner or later!.

**Body and Soul: Wax and Light**

This is a simile for our life. Our bodily existence is like a candle, made up of Nature's elements. It goes back to Nature. It is burnt, buried and decayed. But, in the likeness of the flame, the soul is a divine property. It does not return to Nature. It cannot be burnt, buried or destructed. If you blow out the flame, it is not 'destroyed'. Had it been destroyed, how could you immediately produce it again? The flame that was 'appearing' on the tip of the candle, after blowing out, it 'dissolved' in the ether as a part of fire's property, but the friction of matches can bring it back any moment.

And the flame is not something that diminishes. It has a fixed glow and it will burn with the same glory till the candle exists. However, the candle is melting and the molten wax falls on the earth. It does not go 'up' like the flame. The candle is reducing, diminishing by-and-by and then it finishes. The body is also subject to change, like the candle. It reduces, it diminishes, it becomes frail and feeble and one day it dies. The soul, like the flame, goes to the 'Higher' realm. It has only 'disappeared' from our perception. Hence, there is no question that the journey ends with the end of the body, and that death is the full stop of body. But the life merges into light to re-emerge after another friction.

Thus, the mission of the 'soul' is to 'go up' to its Originator. The mission of the body is to reduce to dust. And even when the "Soul Energy" is dissolved in the Originator, its 'individual probability' is intact. When you burn the candle, the same unlimited and formless fire appears on the wick. When you dip a vessel in the sea, the same vast sea takes the shape of the vessel. Soul and body, God and matter are thus interwoven and inter-expressed. According to the ***'Aitareya Brāhman'***:

***"There is no negation of the sea in the waves and of the waves in the sea; he who knows this, truly knows; he who beholds this, truly beholds; he who lives it, truly lives".***

The form and the formless are but the different dimensions of the same truth. Body and soul both belong to two different realms but together they serve a divine purpose. **Adib Taherzadeh** is a wonderful Baha'i writer who wrote a number of scholarly books including ***"The Revelation of Baha'u'llah"*** in many volumes. In one of his books, he gave a perfect example to reveal the truth of the body and the soul through the example of a tree. We know that tree has its roots deep down in the earth. It is the earth that supplies it food, water and minerals for its growth. But the tree expands its branches towards the sky. Would it not have been seemly for the tree to bow down its branches and intrude into the layers of the earth? If the tree had done so, would it grow?

This physical world and this external life is our sustainer. We get our comfort and nutrients for existence from this world. But our mission is not to get deluded into the depths of this world. We are not just body but a body carrying a soul, and the soul finds its fulfilment in the Supreme Soul, in the same way as all rivers find their fulfilment in the sea. *We must deepen our physical roots in this world where we earn, we live, we act; but our aim and objective is beyond this earth. This is the true meaning of 'detachment' we so miserably misunderstand.*

We are often taught by our so-called 'spiritual' godmen that this life is useless, insipid and we need to attach no value to it. They preach this doctrine in such a way that life seems to be repulsive and worth to be rejected. Such teachings help in nothing but evoking a gloomy, unproductive and 'temporary' approach towards life. What is this teaching if not a direct insult to God? How can we say that the Supreme Artist is great but the art is rubbish? God has not created this world to be treated so abjectly. This world is not a fun-fair that come, play, dance, eat, spit and go away.

In Surah 38 (Sãd), verse 27 of the Holy Quran, Allah has thus exhorted about the significance of our life: **"We did not create the heaven and the earth and everything between them uselessly. Such a view is held only by those who aren't believers.."**

If life had been such a trivial, momentary, non-existent, unwelcoming phenomenon, then it seems illogical why God created it. And if it was created by itself, wonder! How it got such a perfect order? This creation was not a game for God. Again, it is in the Quran:

> *"We did not create the heaven and the earth and everything between them in fun. Had We wanted a recreation, We could find it in Our presence ..."*
>
> (21: 16-17)

How significant this life is becomes clear when we observe the lives of the Messengers of God. Is there any incidence in the life of the Christ that shows his apathy for life? He rather showed utmost love for this world and its people. Wherever that Messiah went, he brought life to the multitudes and healed countless lames and lepers, many a blind and demon-haunted. Mohammad was a perfect trader and an organised general of an uncultured army and, at the same time, a vibrant youth who was keen on reforming the ills of the society. Even Lord Buddha who spent a lot of time in meditation, used to travel far and wide and help people in need by enlightening them. Krishna was one of the most burning examples of a dynamic personality whose love encircled even animals and simple villagers and who taught Arjuna, his disciple, to fight rather than flee. Baha'u'llah was called the "Father of the Poor" because of His deep compassion and love for the downtrodden. He became a vibrant leader of the Babis and kept up their unity in the most disturbed times of a nascent religion. Which Prophet appeared on this earth and turned away from life? Which of them fled to a forest or dwelt on a mountain leaving the people in lurch? They loved life; and showed utmost respect for life. This world offered them nothing but afflictions, tortures, oppositions and denials and yet when the saviour was being crucified, his love-filled lips uttered: ***"Father, forgive them, they know not what they do"***, and the last words of another

Prophet, the Bab, were: ***"The day will come when you will have recognised Me but that day I shall have ceased to be with you"***.

**Life is Rich and Vibrant**

Life is not an "empty dream". Life is a process of an unlimited creation that started in the time immemorial and will go beyond the end that has no end. A major implication of life is that it is reflection of God's love. Love is the only reason for which this universe is created and recreated every moment. What could be any other purpose? Except love all other motives are centripetal. They tend to get everything back to themselves. All centrifugal motives are selfish, self-centred. Love, pure love, is the only centrifugal force of life. It spreads out from its centre to the immensity beyond. It focusses from within to every direction. Only love is a selfless emotion and a 'giving' force of life. God has no need to take anything from us. There is nothing that is unachievable to Him. But He desired to be loved. Thus He split Himself into two: the Lover and the Loved. The Lover part is this world and the Loved part is the Absolute God. This is how "LIFE" came into existence. The Vedic Scriptures basically support Monism which maintains that ***"the ONE became many"*** and the creation came into force.

> *"In the beginning there was no existence. There was no non-existence, too. There was no atmosphere, no sky .... And then a fire sparked in God enkindling love ... the seed of the soul."*
>
> (Rig Veda, 10:129.1-7)

The psychology of true love is based on similarity and equality. The lover sees his or her own image in the beloved. Without this basic property love cannot be called true love. God bestowed the same true love on the mankind. According to the Bible, God created man in His own image. God's love for the creation of men and women can be measured by the fact that He bestowed upon mankind even the LAST attribute that only God had and no other creation could ever possess or could ever dream to have. That is FREE WILL. Except mankind only God has free will. This is the extreme of love! Creating mankind in His image and giving him or her free will has a great implication – it means that **Man can create anything in the same way as God created this universe just out of his desire and thought.** It means that he can use this power to CREATE and he can use this power to DESTROY. Can we find such an example of love on this mortal plane where the lover gave the beloved every authority that he or she himself or herself wielded absolutely?

As we understand from the Holy Quran, the creation of mankind was a matter of supreme felicitation for Allah – Who invited all the angels to prostrate before Adam (signifying that man is even superior to angels) and it became a cause of great envy for Iblis (the Satan) who uttered revenge because Adam was 'honoured above' him. (The Quran, Surah XVII : 61-62).

To conclude, the predominant power of life that it has is because of its expression of divine love. Love is the most adaptable, most forbearing, most resolute, most determined, most dauntless force of the creation. Sharp teeth decay but soft tongue lingers. Stalins and Adolf Hitlers come and go and are thrown in the abyss of the hell of hatred but Gandhis and Martin Luthers are always immortal. The Demon king of Lanka is burnt every Dussehra no matter he lived a golden life and the Rama of love is eternally greeted, no matter he faced a cruel exile. Wars go making a scathing scratch on the beautiful face of peace, but it can never rob life of its power to surmount swords and sing the songs of serenity. Which valley of death can submerge this force of life? Don't you see; even from under the hard crust of the earth, a tiny seed springs forth and it is not just one seed. It is a probability of countless seeds tomorrow! Death, the proud false death can crucify the Christ of Life, but the truth is like Easter. It says, **You can put life in a grave, but it won't stay there. You can nail it to a cross, wrap it in winding sheets and shut it up in a tomb, but it will rise again!** –Clarence W. Hall

❋ ❋

# From Unmanifest to Manifest

> All these beings were unmanifest in the beginning and will be unmanifest after death. Their appearance is only in between.
>
> — *Lord Krishna*

Everything existed 'before', no matter in a manifest or unmanifest form. You, they and I are all a part of God, of this great universe. If it was not so, how could I be created? As fire cannot be ignited and made manifest if it did not exist in the ether in an unmanifest form, I could not be created if I did not 'exist before' in any form.

This preexistence is something that all religions believe in this way or that. However, my purpose is not to burden you with quotations from Books nor I am so versed in them. To be truthful, I personally believe that all religions only refer to a hidden truth and then we ourselves have to discover them. **Osho** has given a wonderful allegory in one of his books 'From Sex to Superconsciousness'.

*One fine morning, a man was enjoying a walk near the seashore. The weather was very pleasant. The wind was laden with sweet smell of flowers and the rippling of the water was producing an enchanting music while birds were flying and chirping over the sea merrily. The sun had just risen and its majestic orange-coloured beams were shining over the water creating a golden charm. The man was overwhelmed. He suddenly remembered that his beloved was ill. She could not come to enjoy this fascinating scenery, but how nice if he could share this life-experience with her! Next morning he came with a box and opened it near the sea so that all the sweet smells, all those dancing beams, those melodious musical notes, freshness and healing touch of the wind could be 'captured' in the box. And he presented this box to his beloved with a great smile of satisfaction. The lady opened the box but there was nothing. No music, no sweetness, no smell, no charm, no freshness. Only the box was there.*

Osho related this allegory to the fact that all religions and their scriptures – Geetā, Bible, Quran, Zendavesta, Tripitak, Guru Granth Sahib, Kitab-i-Aqdas or whatsoever – are just like a 'box' which refers to that 'Sea of Eternity' where we could go and feel that charm and fascination which the 'box' could not contain, even though it sincerely attempted to do so.

**Did I exist before?** This is not a question that needs so much dependence on religious teachings than on our perception and feelings. It is just like someone asking you: "Are you alive?" and your saying: "Wait a minute; let me see in my Scripture". You may be a follower of any religion and refer to your respective Book for specific teachings on this matter but, again, remember the story that went above. No Scripture can give you the "real taste" of Truth till you yourself visit the seashore of eternal life, with eyes open, heart intent and mind unprejudiced. It is just clear that if you exist here (wherever you are sitting or standing or lying just now), it is a natural precedence that "you existed before" somewhere else, in the same way as the Television that is in your room now must have existed before – in the electronics shop, in the factory where all the parts were assembled, in the matters and metals it is made up of, in the mind of the engineer or the scientist who gave it physical shape and, ultimately, in the universe or the Cosmic Mind.

We, too, did exist before. Whether this preexistence of beings was 'manifest' in a bodily form or lay dissolved 'unmanifest' in God (or the Universe) is a different issue. Those who believe that before this birth we were born in some 'form' (in any of the '*yonis*' or species) are people who hold the doctrine of 'poorvajanma' or previous birth. Such people also hold the belief that we will have our next birth in 'body form', i.e., '*punarjanma*' or reincarnation.

Many religions, such as Baha'i Faith hold that the journey of the soul continues even after death but the soul does not assume any such 'body' as our present corporeal body on this earth, we just have a 'heavenly body'. Hinduism itself has varied texts on this philosophical issue and many of them can easily be interpreted to support both the beliefs:

1. that we had a 'bodily' existence before our present life and our 'bodily' existence will continue even after this life till we have our final consummation with our Greater Self (*Parmātmā* or God), and

2. that we have an unmanifest existence before as we were the part of '*Parmātmā*' and after death we will dissolve in the same *Parmātmā* and thus 'continue to live'.

**Body and the Purpose**

'Body' explained and understood in all the religious connotations baffles our mind for one simple fact that we have a 'certain pre-image of body'. When we see our hands and feet, mouth and ears, eyes and nose then we develop an 'image' of body. Whether we have a 'spiritual body' or a 'physical body' after death is not important but what is important is that 'we have a body'. A body can be in any form but it has 'senses' and that's why it is body. If the objectives of these 'senses' are perceived, then who cares if the body is 'spiritual' or 'physical'? We see many creatures on the earth itself with different body shapes and different functional capacities. Snakes do not 'hear' through ears. Some say that their 'eyes' listen. If we will study the lives of plants and animals, we will be amazed by the wonderful findings. Some trees even 'sing' though they have no 'lips'. Fishes breathe through their gills, not 'nostrils'.

In my childhood, when I used to see my family members offering 'naivedya' (food offering) to 'Gods' I wondered how could they eat? But believing that they must be 'eating' as my aunts say so, I had no hesitation in stealing away some laddoos at night from the divine share. But once I was suspected and slapped, and when I innocently claimed that 'God' might have eaten, I was advised that 'Gods' don't need to eat with mouth; they just 'smell' the food and it is 'consumed'. Now, this may be truth or balderdash, it suggests that in some body forms 'smell' can replace the function of 'taste'. If so, a spiritual body can also have 'senses' to satisfy the 'urges'. Our dreams are a flagrant example. In dreams, our 'physical body' never goes anywhere away from the bed we are sleeping on, but a 'subtle body' is able to travel to the sky, the mountains, far-off places, and meet people, eat and drink, feel and act everything as 'real'! When the truth is so evident, why is there so much dissension on the term 'body'?

The purpose of a 'body' is expressed through its 'senses'. For example, in bodily existence we have the power of hearing, feeling, walking, smelling, tasting, etc. and these 'senses' are served by 'sense organs' like ears, fingers, legs, nose, tongue, etc. But God can make these senses independent of any organs. He Himself does not need any organ for His infinite functions. **"He walks without legs, hears without any ears. He performs countless acts without any hands. Having no need of mouth, He enjoys all tastes. With no need of tongue, He is the superb Speaker"**. – (in Ramcharitamanas, by Tulsidas). All that it means is this much that body is a broad term.

We can have any form of 'body' but if it is true, as the description of Heaven and Hell are given in 'Books', that there are gardens of delight, fairies of innocent beauty, angels of matchless charm, foods of delectable varieties, drinks of indescribable sweetness, companions of unbending faithfulness, rivers warbling and bulbuls chirping, then it must also be true that to see, feel, hear and taste these things, some form of 'body' needs to be there. In the same way, if there is no 'body' then who has problem with the scorching fire of the hell?

Then, those who do not believe in life before and after, will boldly say, as they always say, that there is no hell or heaven. This is only a 'mental state' of delight and grief that is symbolised as heaven and hell respectively. In this way, they at least accept that our 'mind' can also serve as a 'body' which feels delight and grief. And if we further believe in their un-heavenly belief, everything that is said in the Quran and other Scriptures, including writings of the latest religion of this age – the Baha'i Faith, is just eyewash. God and

His Prophets showed us a '*sabz bagh*' a green pasture as our 'leaders' show us! There are no rivers warbling, no faithful companions, no meetings with our dear ones, no eternal trees and unfading flowers. These were all high-flown campaigns of God's advertisement department! Really, when logic becomes too prudent, it becomes very foolish!

This is not my point to dwell further on the matter of heaven and hell. My only point is to say that we always have a body or a form – for the simple fact that it is body and form that proves we are not 'partners with God' but a separate Form in the Formless. If we had no 'body' as our individual identity, we were going to be 'merged' into God's identity and, thus, be a 'partner with Him'. A drop is not a partner with the Sea for the simple fact that the drop is in the Sea. If the drop had not been in the Sea, it would have been the Sea itself!

**Earlier Existence**

The point is: **Did we really exist before as an 'individual being' – as John and Christina, Ramesh and Nina, Saleem and Zena, etc.?** Based on my belief in the '*Karma*' (Cause and Effect) theory, I feel "YES". The prime factor of my belief is this: Every individual is born on this planet in a different surrounding, mostly too much in contrast with each other. These different surroundings play not only a vital but decisive role in shaping the life, destiny, actions, habits, knowledge and achievements of the respective individuals. Some are born in a very rich country, to rich parents, in greatly supportive environments. Things go easier for them in a natural way. They face no or little struggle in finding their love, occupation, wealth, opportunities and other achievements. Others are born at a poor place, to impoverished parents, in a highly conflicting atmosphere. Their whole life is spent in arduous struggles. They utterly fail in love no matter how sincere they were, have poor income no matter however willing and endeavouring they are, and have to toil too much for small achievements.

The question is: **Is the birth of a person in a good or bad 'environment' just a matter of chance, a result of merely biological, social or economic consequences?** Is it just that I was 'conceived' in an embryo as a foetus and that's all? If yes, either we are not "created" and just 'toppled down' through a sexual process in a haphazard manner, or the Creator does not seem to be very just and humane. It can be compared to an organised race of people, horses, cars or anything in which all the participants of the race stand at distinctive distances: some quite ahead, some far behind; and the referee blows his whistle and the race starts. What is the validity of such a race if the first winner is the person who was on forefront and the defeated fellow is clearly the one who stood kilometres away from him? If God is such a Referee, He is unacceptable. It is not possible that He is a true Judge, the One Who loves all equally, wants the welfare of everyone and then puts each one, in this race-ground of life, at such respective contrasts as can decide one's success and failure. A boy born in an igloo on a remote snow-covered land of Antarctica can surely not compare his efficiency with a boy born in Los Angeles with his mother being someone like Angelina Jolie. It is unbelievable that God (if He exists) left each individual just to the mercy of a mechanical device, subject to the laws of sex and biology, and when the individual was born He said "Ok! Now as you came somehow, I love you". If I was a part of God "before", how come He forgot His part and left it to a blind and randomised system of birth? Either I was not a part of God if the process of my birth was so 'careless' or there must be a 'careful' selection for my birth on this planet.

If we believe that this great universe is in a meticulous order, in perfect harmony with a far-reaching purpose, it also leads us to believe that in such an orderly, harmonised and purposeful creation, my own birth as John or Christina, Ramesh or Nina, Saleem or Zena was not left as subject to randomised biological laws. Again, this process can be compared to the work of assembling a computer or a car or any complicated machine. The process of assembling or manufacturing a high level product is surely a 'genius' act, a systematic business. We cannot say that one part of such a delicate machine was not part of the 'system' or 'point of attention' of the manufacturer. It was just fixed somehow or not enough care was given to its fitting. If this universe is so complicated and yet so systematic, it cannot be assumed that the birth of an individual was just a 'bye-product' of this entire genius system. Someone chose to have sex and I was somehow born. No, not so. In other words, I was not born just because I was conceived in my mother's womb, by my father's semen, under fertile conditions, and that was all. If I am the result of such a haphazard system, I feel very unlucky if I am living in an abject condition, and I feel so proud if I am born with a silver spoon in the mouth.

Religions tell us that God has given us 'freedom of choice' or 'free will'. How unjust He was if He gave me all 'freedom' only after making me a 'slave' at the very initial point, after making me a 'victim' of an accidental birth! What is the value of such a 'free will' which is based on negligence of the first vital 'free will' that could affect my whole life and its choices? Is it not like telling a slave that you have a complete 'free will' except this that you are my slave?

God cannot be unjust, nor will He decide my present birth just through an inert biological law. Therefore, it seems logical to me that my birth in a prosperous or an abject 'environment' was my own 'free will' expressed through my previous '*karma*'. And since I need a 'bodily' form to perform my '*karma*', **I must surely have had a 'bodily' form before**.

### Karma and Free Will

Here the correlation of '*Karma*' and 'free will' needs to be explained as many people see both these terms as contradictory ones. It is defined that our '*Karma*' is composed of three parts: 'Sanchit' or stored *karma*, '*Prārabdh*' or destined karma, and '*Kriyamān*' or active *karma*. God bestowed free will since the beginning that has no beginning. Take the story of **Adam** and **Eve**, the 'first' human creatures according to the Bible and the Quran. They both lived in the Garden of Eden. Their '*karma*' had not yet started to that point. God told them to live in the Garden to their utmost satisfaction and partake of everything they had there except the fruits of a certain tree. God even warned them that the result of touching that forbidden tree would not be good. However, since God had bestowed 'free will' upon them, they 'chose' to partake of those forbidden fruits. Thus, their Karmic Cycle started.

The moment they 'chose' to perform this act of 'touching' the forbidden tree, the '*Kriyamān*' (active) *karma* went in operation. As a result, they were 'expelled' from the heaven. The earth, on which they were thrown down, was the 'condition' or 'consequence' or 'effect' they received as their share of '*Prārabdh*' (destined) *karma*, i.e., they made their own destiny by acting in a certain way. If they had 'chosen' to act in a way harmonious with God and had not 'touched the forbidden fruits', their '*karma*' would have been positive and the 'consequence' was sure to be 'heaven'.

Well, now after learning a lesson from their own folly, they might have decided to act in a positive way. When their actions or '*kriyamān karma*' would be positive, the '*prārabdh karma*' or their destiny would also be good and when they die, some of the good '*karma*' for which time did not allow to reap the benefits would accompany them in the 'next life' as part of their 'Sanchit' (stored) *karma*. It is clear that the 'free will' comes first. '*Karma*' is nothing but exercised free will. Therefore, it is always possible to change the consequences of '*karma*' through the exercise of powerful thoughts leading to intensive actions.

Nobody expelled Adam and Eve from the Garden but it means that when we 'disobey' a divine rule, we fall from our station to a degraded level. God is not present here in a physical form to tell us what to do and what not to do. But He has put inspirations inside our own pure conscience to tell us what is 'good' and what is 'bad', what can be 'partaken of' and what is 'forbidden'. The 'purity' of conscience is essential for that inner guidance. That is what Baha'u'llah, the Founder of Baha'i Faith, put forth in the very first order of "**The Hidden Words**":

**O son of Spirit! My first counsel is this: possess a pure, kindly and radiant heart that thine may be a sovereignty ancient, imperishable and everlasting.**

It is evident that I had a previous existence because I exist 'now'. 'Now' comes from a previous point, however subtle it may be. And since we have been designated specific birth conditions, it is because of our own 'choice' or '*karma*'. *God has not done any injustice.* It is we who brought ourselves forward to this level where we are now. It is equally true that we can carry ourselves forward to any desired direction we want in the future lives. This journey will continue. 'This' life and 'that' life is only 'our' conception. In the constant flow of eternity, there is no 'before' and 'after', neither life nor death. What we call 'death' is nothing but an allusion, a name given to the 'nameless', the 'extreme of one particular life', our gateway to the next existence. According to Ludwig Josef J. Wittgenstein, **"Death is not an event in life ... not a fact in the world"**.

❋ ❋

5

# The Myriad Worlds

> Verily I say, the creation of God embraceth worlds besides this world, and creatures apart from these creatures. In each of these worlds He hath ordained things which none can search except Himself.
>
> — *Baha' u' llah*

It is not necessary that my previous life must have flourished on this same planet, the earth. There may be myriad 'earths' of God, many earth-like or different planets. In the same way, my body could be in any form, far unimaginable from our earthly body, but I must have been given means and ways to 'act', to exercise my 'free will', to perform my '*karma*', to think, to do right or wrong. There also I must have had a conscience, and may be even Messengers and Scriptures, to show me the way to the shore of eternity where fresh wind is blowing and pleasing smells enthral the soul. Similarly, after this life I will go to 'different' worlds of God (or return to this earth, depending on the inscrutable wisdom of the Creator) and may assume different 'bodily' forms; be they heavenly or corporeal. If the results of my '*karma*' are not fully reaped off, I have all reasons to believe that I will not 'cease' to be because **energy must express itself**.

It is clear that you and me as individuals are not the product of chances. We did exist before in the form of a 'doer' and will exist as a 'doer' even after this life, till our salvation, i.e., the mingling of our individual soul with the Supreme Soul. There is no question whether we existed or will further exist on this same earth or in the countless other worlds of God. In fact, considering the vastness, immenseness, infinity and illimitability of the creation, this question is as foolish as a king's son asking on his birthday if he should wear the last year's maroon dress or one of the new apparels bought recently. A king's son never asks such foolish questions and picks up whatever he wants to. But those who have few dresses need to ask such a question often. God has created a vast and expansive cosmos full of numerous worlds, galaxies, stars and planets, and we are still ignorant of those many worlds. This earth on which we breathe is actually so small in comparison to this entire universe that perhaps even a dot cannot display its status, and yet we feel so proud that this is the only planet where life exists!

### Life on other Planets

Many scientists are still puzzled with the question whether life is possible on some planet other than the earth or not. Till now they have explored only few 'places' of our own galaxy. They have explored the Moon and the Mars, to be specific. Findings are very limited to prove or disprove that even these handfuls of extra-terrestrial places are 'fit for life' or not. Maybe the scientists of some 'other worlds' (the aliens) have, simultaneously, sent their aircrafts on the earth which might have landed on the Antarctica and they might have summed up in their science journals that the earth is not a place 'fit for life' as it is solely covered with snow. Or maybe their spacecrafts glided on the Atlantic or the Pacific, leading them to conclusion that the earth is not a 'liveable' planet because it is only water.

We must admit that we have a very shallow knowledge of this great universe so far and we are in no way able to conclude that this earth is the only place fit for life. On the other hand, our knowledge of the life-fostering factors is just relative to our own planet. We have no other experience of possible lives. For example, if there is no air on the Mars, we are prone to jump on this inference that 'life is not possible on the Mars since there is no oxygen and no life is possible without oxygen'. In fact, such conclusions will only prove our own insufficiency of knowledge in understanding the depth and diversity of this universe. Don't we see on this earth itself that creatures living in different conditions are adapted to diverse ecological circumstances? Fish breathe in the water where very little oxygen is available. Some species of fish live in snow-covered lakes and yet they thrive on very little oxygen. The plant kingdom does not even need oxygen to breathe in. They inhale carbon dioxide and exhale oxygen, a wisdom of Nature to recycle the life-air necessary for our existence on this planet. We see amazing examples of adaptability in creatures found across this globe. Chameleons change their skin colour to hide in their surrounding. Feeding habits are also surprisingly different. Pigs and wild animals feed on rotten things, meat and some dirtiest possible food and they still remain healthy. If we, the human beings, consume such 'foods', we will die of infection. From these diverse varieties of life-patterns, is it still difficult to guess that if God has so planned, He can create "living conditions" quite different from that of the earth? Thus, life can be possible in any of those countless worlds.

**Many Dimensions**

The reality of dimensions, wavelength and so on, and all these too need to be properly understood. We can see things because they appear before us in the specified dimensions. Our sight and hearing capacity have their limits. Some creatures like hawk can see farther than us. Many reptiles 'hear' from their skin rather than their ears. The wavelength of sound is fixed differently for different creature. Some creatures are so sensitive and receptive to far-off sound-waves that they even show special behaviours to predict natural disasters like an earthquake or a cyclone. Many animals can see things in dark that we can't see. Maybe, some of them can see things or hear sounds beyond the dimensions specified for human beings. Who knows!

Ants can hear subtler sounds than we can do, and birds might be able to see more hidden dimensions than we can. It is also possible that other 'spirits', angels and fairies might be living within this same world but we can't see them!

Our known dimensions are only the length, width and height. Einstein referred to Time and Space also as dimensions. Some say that Symmetry is yet another dimension. Modern scientists working in the field of Quantum Gravitation now authentically declare that there are many more dimensions hidden from our senses. As of now, more than 10 dimensions are 'believed' to exist, and they say the list is not final! Why we can't 'see' those hidden dimensions is only because God has restricted us to these 'known' dimensions only. Just consider an ant moving on a piece of paper. It can only know left and right, to and fro, just two dimensions, because it cannot 'leave' the newspaper to explore it up and down. In the same way, we can know 'other dimensions' only when we can 'leave' the levels of our known 3 dimensions, and that we cannot do! According to the 'String Theory' of the scientists, there are several dimensions beyond this three-dimensional level. We can't 'see' them but the law of gravitation helps to 'feel' them.

In a nutshell, God is not bound to create only such worlds of existence which are visible to our earthly eyes, but once we are placed in such worlds we will know their reality. A foetus in the womb is hardly some millimetres away from this earthly world but if we somehow try and tell that foetus that its distance from a wonderful world is only this much, would it believe?

God, as we assume Him to be, is Pure and Sinless. He is Brilliant and full of Splendour. Therefore, no soul can intermingle with Him till it has freed itself from the entire bondage of '*karma*', be they good or evil. Many people believe that good *karma* leads us to meeting with God, but according to the Geeta, even good *karma*, if not performed in a 'detached mode', cannot bring our final emancipation. Still we have to be born. This is because of the "energy of desire" we have released. The only way to our salvation in such a condition when the flow of '*karma*' is still in effect is the mercy of God Himself. Prayers of our sincere ones can also help in evoking God's mercy and thus freeing us from the bondage of the cycle of birth and rebirth. This is because God is above His laws. He is not bound by the 'law of *karma*' but the 'law of *karma*' is bound by His permission. God will not generally violate His own laws or act for us beyond the ambit of His laws because it will create chaos in the world, but if He wants, He can do so. That is why we have "prayers for forgiveness" in all religions. If only the 'law' had to rule and God's mercy had no interceptive effect, what is the use of a prayer for forgiveness? Law is inert, it does not 'forgive' or 'punish' anyone.

Life exists before and will exist further in its appropriate shape and form. 'How' and 'Where' is not a question of our realm.

* *

## 6

# In the Ocean of Eternity

*Oh! in that future let us think*
*To hold each heart - the heart that shares*
*With them the immortal waters drink*
*And soul in soul grow deathless theirs!*

*— Lord Byron*

Even the majority of those who do not believe in any previous birth, believe that the individual soul 'existed before' as an inseparable entity of the Supreme Soul. They only deny the possibility of a 'bodily' form of existence, i.e., the soul's existence in an individual entity.

The first thing that is vital and essential to understand is that everything and everyone existed in God as an 'individual identity'. This creation is nothing separate from God and nothing beyond, above or exclusive of Him. Whatever exists already exists in Him in countless forms, modes and designs. Why we cannot understand this truth is because of the inability of our own imagination. To understand how many things impose 'limits' on our mind and imagination, just read this sentence:

**Thinking Beyond Known Facts**

**Some 2 pixogellion years ago, V saw a broad-minded amoeba loving a greek princess in the 2050, and the princess said in her ecstasy: 'diddo ... duan sot minz pelj dhyet' as she reclined on her watery couch.**

Make a list of everything that 'troubles' your imagination in the above sentence and why? The amoeba ... the Greek princess ... love .... the language used by her .... her 'watery' couch .... and who is 'V' who made all the amalgamation of time ... what is pixogellion? All this make a mess in our mind and we reject it. We are comfortable with things that we already know in the ambit of our time and space. We have a pre-fixed image of amoeba, of the standard parameters of time measurement such as minute, second and light-years, of languages that exist, behaviours that are okay, and so many things. Thus, the above sentence will seem strange and even unacceptable. Our imagination is also determined by the known numerical, qualitative and quantitative set-patterns. However, the cosmos in which we live is free from all barriers and definitive limits whatsoever.

These are the limits of time and space, numbers and dimensions, shapes and sizes, etc., that impede our imagination to picture our individual identity in the Supreme Entity of this universe. However, as this physical world contains everything that is in the spiritual realm, it is not difficult to understand the divine truths. The truth that is gaining popularity in modern times is that there are several parallel worlds. It being so, we are in a position to understand today that we did not only really exist before as an 'individual being' – as John and Christina, Ramesh and Nina, Saleem and Zena, etc. – but that there are many Johns and Christinas, Rameshes and Ninas, Saleems and Zenas.

It will be so exciting to know for you that at the same time when you are reading this book, so many other versions of 'you' are doing some other things in their respective multiverses. It is difficult to believe because you have a pre-defined knowledge that 'you' can be only one. If I tell you that while you are on this planet 'Earth', weighing some 60 kilogrames, another version of 'yours' on an unknown planet (say, 'Mirth') weighs hardly 5 kilogrames, would you believe? And would you believe that though you are a shy and gentle person as a reader of this book, your so many other versions in the parallel worlds reflect dramatically diverse characters in which you are violent, rude, disobedient, warm, open, careless, passionate, homesick, effeminate, etc.?

**Different Worlds and Life**

According to the Hindu *Purānas*, there is an infinite number of universes. The reality of many worlds and replicas of our existence has revealed itself, for the observation of human being, since ancient times and has driven many novelists and writers, such as **Jorge**

**Luis Borges** (*The Garden of Forking Paths*), **H. G. Wells** (*Time Machine*), **Douglas Adams** (*Mostly Harmless*), **John Wyndham** (*Random Quest*), **C. S. Lewis** (*The Chronicles of Narnia*), **Poul Anderson** (*Operation Chaos*), **Eric Flint** (*1632*), **Frederik Pohl** (*The Coming of the Quantum Cats*), **Jonathan Swift** (*Gulliver's Travels*), **H. P. Lovecraft** (*Dream Cycle*), and so on. In "*The Garden of Forking Paths*", Borges imagines a world where things take place in infinitely parallel ways. In "*Random Quest*", a laboratory experiment sends the character of the novel in a parallel universe where the Second World War had never happened.

The recent findings of science in quantum mechanics have added a veritable significance to this idea of "**many worlds, many existences**" or even better known as "**Hyperspace**" in many fictions. In the language of quantum mechanics simplified, "Parallel Universes" stand on the basis of the truth that every possible outcome of every event exists in its own "history" or "world". Everything that could possibly have happened in our past but didn't occurred in the past of some other universe or universes. This is a universe full of 'probabilities' and each probability is a world in itself.

Take for example a computer program - Microsoft Word. Microsoft Word is only one program, no matter on how many computers it is installed. Yet, it functions with immense probabilities, not only on different computers but even on our own PC. The operator, on his/her PC, can execute countless instances of Microsoft

Word: one for drafting a letter, another for making a list, yet another for script-writing perhaps. The same Microsoft Word can be maximised, minimised and used through several Windows. And each "file" is different: different name, different contents, different nature, different wordings, and yet it is the same Microsoft Word expressing in diversities. The only limit can be imposed by the hard drive and the RAM. However, the CPU of this universe has an immensely copious hard drive and unlimited memory-packed RAM. The individual soul of John or Christina, Ramesh or Nina, Saleem or Zena is like a God-programmed Microsoft Word and on different monitors or windows (worlds), its several instances can run.

The phenomenon of "many worlds" is a reality in keeping with the law of abundance that permeates our universe. The expression of life is so rich and varied that it needs more than one universe, not only for its consecutive unfoldment in the form of reincarnation, but also in the form of simultaneous ramification. A simple logical basis for the multiple universe (or parallel universe or many worlds) is found in the well-established laws of physical gravity, law of attraction and other laws concerning energy, its indestructibility, and the various modes it takes in order to release its potency. Newton's simple law that **"For every action, there is an equal and opposite reaction"** is said easier than realised in the complex order of human desires. Given that each strong desire is a potential energy, it is bound to stir the atoms towards actions and reactions.

However, each action and reaction cannot be fulfilled or placed within a given time and space because it may lead to collisions.

For example, it is easy to understand the third law of Newton if a ball is thrown against a wall. We know the ball will bounce back. But imagine a circular room (because we know this universe is oval or circular) with walls all around, and a million balls of desires by millions of people being hurled towards the wall. Imagine the dynamism, rapidity and multiplicity of the actions and reactions: a million balls of desires hurled, a million reactions in the form of bouncing back of desire-balls, their echoing and bouncing effects in the universe! Imagine the commotion and confusion so complicated in nature and volume that adjusting and balancing them will only be too necessary.

**Desires: Strong, Impulsive and Shifting**

This is what God does by shifting some desires to other realms of fruitions. Some desires are sent in the powerful world of dreams where they find their expressions. However, some desires are so strong and impulsive that they cannot be satisfied in dreams nor during this lifetime. They are shifted to next lives of the individual. Some desires are immediate but impossible to be met out in this current world and they are transferred to a parallel world.

Many desires are not expressed in the realms of reality of this world because of lack of opportunities or other reasons. So what? A bullet charged from a pistol equipped with silencer is also equally powerful as a bullet charged from a normal pistol. Desires unfulfilled are always hovering in a form of energy and they need a vent; always!

There are many expressions of love that remained deep in our subconscious. There are many desires we could not fulfil. Human mind soars in diverse worlds of imagination: worlds that are wider than reality. These "many worlds" give space to these imaginations and urgent aspirations unable to be contained in the world we live in. For example, a person can cherish a very strong desire to see Mahatma Gandhi and talk to him face to face. One out of those thousands of people, who might have heard about the beauty of **Marilyn Monroe** and her romance with **Mr. Kennedy**, may foster an unquenchable thirst to see that matchless beauty of her time and talk to Mr. Kennedy about his experiences with that charming lady. One may want to spend his time in a world where **Omar Khayyam**, the great Persian poet, still sings his immortal *Rubbaiyat*, or dive in that depth of time when **Bach** was composing the best of his musical pieces. A soul may also yearn earnestly to float ahead on the streams of time and see the picture of the planet Earth a hundred years from now.

**Reality vs Preceptions**

We are socially and genetically programmed to believe that we must live in reality and not in dreams, and, therefore, everything described above will be nullified by a 'realist' person. It can easily be said that nobody can meet M.K. Gandhi now because he is dead. Now that world is gone where Marilyn Monroe bewitched Kennedy with her charm, and that world can never be 'actualised' now.

Yet, the same 'realists' will readily agree that everything we see around as 'real' did not exist a hundred or a thousand years ago. If they existed anywhere, it was in the human mind as 'dreams', and from that 'aerial' world of ideas they alighted on the runway of reality.

The same 'realists' will also attest to the truth that nothing exists in this external world as a viable 'matter'. Everything exists as a perception in mind. No truth exists outside the individual mind. Every colour, smell, feeling, visual object, sound, or whatever can be named, is an 'individual experience in one's mind' and thus a truth has a billion versions from individual to individual. In brief, there is no 'reality' in real sense! There are only 'perceptions'.

And the universe is open to allow all perceptions. It has a smooth pitch for every dream to fly, every feeling to slide, every thought to float, and, within this universe a 'multiverse' is possible for each individual, so that each desire, even if conflicting in a given world, can be materialised in some 'other' world.

For example, John loves Brita very dearly but Brita is lost in Jimmy's love, while Jimmy has no feelings for Brita but for Beatrice, though Beatrice loves John. Now, if each one, John (for Brita), Brita (for Jimmy), Jimmy (for Beatrice), and Beatrice (for John), is truly sincere, passionate, powerful and faithful in his or her love, and if it is true that all strong desires are energies that must find their match under the 'Law of Attraction', what possibilities are there? In this 'real' world, if John is matched with Beatrice, it is good for Beatrice but not for John; if Beatrice is matched with Jimmy, it is good for Jimmy but not for Beatrice; and so on. Therefore, a parallel world is to be created where John can feel and perceive Brita as his lover and for Brita a parallel world is created where she lives with Jimmy. Thus, in this 'parallel world', there are no conflicts as in the 'real' world.

The truth is that whatever we truly believe becomes our reality, and in that reality each desire is fulfilled. This is the promise of this boundless universe, provided we trust and follow our bliss. If John loves Brita truly and sets no other 'alternative' for Brita in his mind, he will surely find Brita, no matter whatever realities of Brita are. **Realities follow dreams, dreams do not follow reality**.

**Preception, Imagination and Dreams**

In fact, the world of dream in which we go easily so often when we sleep, is itself a connection with so many worlds and dimensions of our existence: past and future. In dreams we see such places as we have never seen before, meet such people whom we never met before in this life, experience such feelings which are so close to our longing soul and yet we never felt them on this earth! And we dream all these things when our "physical body" is but lying on a couch, unable to go anywhere!

> *Indeed, O Brother, if we ponder each created thing, we shall witness a myriad perfect wisdoms and learn a myriad new and wondrous truths. One of the created phenomena is the dream. Behold how many secrets are deposited therein, how many wisdoms treasured up, how many worlds concealed. Observe, how thou art asleep in a dwelling, and its doors are barred; on a sudden thou findest thyself in a far-off city, which thou enterest without moving thy feet or wearying thy body; without using thin e eyes, thou seest; without taxing thine ears, thou hearest; without a tongue, thou speakest. And perchance when ten years are gone, thou wilt witness in the outer world the very things thou hast dreamed tonight.*
>
> (Baha'u'llah, The Seven Valleys)

We say God is All-embracing but do we really think what it means? If today something 'new' is produced, how could He be All-embracing? It simply means that "new" things keep on coming and He embraces them. He is not "already" All-embracing then. In that case, His attribute as All-embracing is something to be conceived under Darwinian 'Theory of Evolution'. An aeroplane is made in 18th Century and God embraces it! In 19th Century internet is discovered and then God embraced it! M.K. Gandhi was born in 1869 and embraced by God then? Hitler was born in 1889 and then God embraced him? Very poor and *bechāra* is God if He depends on things to 'happen' first and then 'own' them!

**Everything in and from Brahma**

In the 11th chapter of Geetā, Lord Krishna gives Arjuna, his disciple, a glimpse of His immense Being. Arjuna was able to see in Him all creatures and all sorts of existences appearing and disappearing: **That time Arjuna saw in the body of Lord Krishna many a diverse world assembled in a place** (Geeta, 11:13) and spoke to Him:

> *O Lord! I see in Your body all the Gods and clusters of various beings, the Brahma on his lotus-seat, Mahadev, great seers and celestial serpents.*
>
> (Geetā, 11:15)

*Pashyāmi devām stava deva dehe*
*Sarvām stathā bhuta vishesh sanghān,*
*Brahmanām isham kamalāsantha*
*Mrishinshcha sarva anurāngāshcha divyān.*

Brahma includes the Trinity: *Brahmā, Vishnu* and *Mahādev* (also named Shiva) make up the 'Trinity' of Hindu theology representing, respectively, the three inherent powers of 'God' as 'Generator', 'Organiser' and 'Destroyer'.

God is the eternal ocean of 'Super Consciousness' in which countless bubbles of 'conscious' entities are born and decayed; and are born again. This is just a 'Night and Day Phenomenon'. In each bubble, the ocean represents its essential elements though in a microcosm. To say that bubbles are 'born' and they 'die' is just a linguistic expression used for layman's convenience. Otherwise, the truth is that bubbles always exist in the ocean in the form of 'probability'. Whatever we are or think we were in the said 'past' or can be in the so-called 'future', whatever we can think of, imagine, surmise, infer, induce, suppose or presume are all 'existing' in the Super Consciousness as 'possibilities'; and even countless instances of one single possibility. If I can think I was John or Christina, Ramesh or Nina, Saleem or Zena, it simply means I did exist as such because I cannot think anything beyond the Super Conscious probability. And if I think I did not exist as John or Christina, Ramesh or Nina, Saleem or Zena, still I did exist as such because this very imagination of 'not being a form or a body' is, in itself, the proof of being so; again; because we cannot think anything beyond the Super Conscious probability. In saying that "there is a chair" and in saying that "there is no chair", in both ways the 'chair' exists.

Thus, if something existed in the form of 'probability', it also existed in the form of 'reality' because each probability is an 'unmanifested reality'. As in the ocean, each rippling wave existed before the forces of the wind caused the ripples; as in the desert, each sand particle existed as an individual sand particle of the desert; as in an apple, the numerous seeds of innumerable apples lay hidden to spring forth in the span of the 'future'; as in the snow-layers of the Himalayas, it was preordained that a certain drop of melting ice will go into the Ganges while another drop will be drifted by a puff of the wind to become a drop in Huang-Ho, so was I 'clandestine' in my Creator as John and Christina, Ramesh and Nina, Saleem and Zena. As **Thomas Boston** said: **"None can comprehend eternity but the eternal God. Eternity is an ocean, whereof we shall never see the shore; it is a depth where we can find no bottom; a labyrinth from whence we cannot extricate ourselves and where we shall never lose the door."**

* *

# The Beginning that has no Beginning

*In the beginning was the Word and the Word was with God. .... All things were made through Him, and without Him nothing was made that was made.*

*— The Bible, John: 1: 1,3*

When the light of the Sun is cast on the darksome world, everything appears clear. Every wise observer knows that everything 'exists', the light of the Sun only 'reveals' or 'manifests' them. When the light of the Soul is shed over existence, it is visible, otherwise it is invisible. This is just like rotation of the earth on its axis. When India has sunlight, Canada is dark. It does not mean that Canada does not exist during a particular period.

Lord Krishna exhorts His disciple Arjuna:

*It's not that you, me and these kings did not exist before, nor it is true that we will cease to be hereafter.*

(Geetā, 2:12)

*Na tvewāham gatu nāsam na tvam neme ganādhipāh;*
*Na chaiva na bhavishyāmah sarve vayamatah param.*

**Karma: Cause and Effect**

People who do not believe in previous life existence or the Theory of *Karma* (The Law of Cause and Effect), have a very popular argument that goes like this – **'If this life (birth) is a consequence of the previous 'karma', what 'karma' the first man did that he was sent on this earth?'**

The question needs to be answered from many angles. First, this life is not just a reward or a punishment following the 'karmic cycle'. God has a free choice for creation. If He is bound by a certain law all the time, how is He God? God has made laws for order and organisation, but He is not a subject to His own laws. Moreover, if '*karma*' had been the only reason for this creation, how could this exquisite life of the flora and fauna exist? How these picturesque valleys and mountains would have been created? The serene blue oceans, the warbling rivers, these lush-green meadows, how could they come into existence? What '*karma*' was performed by these inanimate or intention-free objects? Only those can 'act', follow the path of right or wrong, virtue or sin, who possess free will and analytical wisdom. God has not bestowed free will and wisdom on any other creature than man. No doubt, a little amount of instinctive free will and wisdom is inherent even in small creatures like an ant, but that is only for the purpose of their survival. No other creature can understand the nature of the soul, why it is born and what reward or punishment could be hidden in its existence. Had this world been created only by the Karmic theory, we had never witnessed any other creature but mankind.

The second point arising from the above argument is about the '*karma*', the so-called 'first man' did. Even though it is clear that God has not created this world for rewarding and punishing people according to their respective '*karma*', it is also true that each human being is born in the very matrix of his or her *karma* and tastes the fruits of his or her deeds. '*Karma*' is a Law and not the Purpose of this creation. It is like the fact that all planets of the solar system revolve round the Sun but it will be a folly to conclude that the planets are made only to circle round the Sun. The planets are there for various functions that would effect the order of the universe, but for these 'functions' they need to revolve round the Sun.

However, if we strongly believe that '*Karma*' is the only reason for our birth, it must be asked what the fault of the 'first man' was. Now, if Adam and Eve were the 'first' to be sent on this earth, we know that they did something to initiate the 'cycle of *karma*'. God is not faulty. They used their free will in disobedience and partook of the forbidden fruit. Therefore, it was their own '*karma*' that shaped their destiny and that of the mankind.

Nonetheless, the very basic fabrication of this question is green. 'First' and 'last' and all numerical suppositions in between are based on our perception of time. But does Time exist? Time exists only in our comparative feeling of a continuum. Time is an imaginary child of our memory. We know it is 'now' because we have a memory of 'now that just flows by'. Hadn't our mind had the power of recession, Past could not be possible. Hadn't our mind had the power of progression, Future could not exist. Even Space is a comparative allusion, measured in terms of time and distance and limited by our own incapacities. Madrid is far from Paris only because of the aeroplane taking some 2 hours to cover this distance. If we would be able to increase the plane's speed to 1000 kmph, there would be almost no distance between Madrid and Paris.

**Human Limitations**

We have our own limits, we have our own incapacities, we have demarcations of time and space, but is the Super Conscious also barred by these considerations? Don't we see that the very elements of life and energy know no bounds of time and distance? In a few seconds, light travels a million miles. The radio waves, electricity, the pictures on our television, the voices on our phones are all instantaneously present anywhere and anytime. Then why is it difficult for us to grasp the truth of time-less-ness and space-less-ness when it comes to the operation of the Divine Will? What's this foolishness of 'first' and 'last'? We can't even solve the simple problem if it was egg in the beginning or the chicken, but we dare to step in the Sea of Eternity and brag to catch the 'first' fish? We cannot even point out on our own orange-shaped earth which is the first country and which is the last, but we venture to figure out the 'first' man that God created!

There is nothing first and there is nothing last. These are 'counting games' of a kindergarten child. The divine child lives in the eternity and for him each moment is a flow of 'now' a constant flow of consciousness that knows no limit, no bounds, no imaginary scales on the map of perpetuation.

Time is a conception or an illusion in our own mind and expression of our own limits. This can be understood by an illustration. Watch a tiny ant moving on the floor around you. What is the ambit of Past, Present or Future for this small creature? Hardly 5-6 inches! From where it is moving now, it can hardly see 5-6 inches ahead. That's its Present time and space, and beyond this is Future because it cannot see that! Now, this ant is passing through many turn-points of that small place. A bigger insect is waiting to devour it on the next turn-point, just 5 inches from where the ant is now. Does the ant know about the insect? A danger just 5 inches away is 'unforeseeable' to the poor creature! But you seated in your chair and observing everything, experience it all as an episode of 'Now'. You know that the ant is to be devoured by the insect. The same 'you' - when in an aircraft - have even a wider overview of your Present. In the span of a few seconds, you can see the whole of a city like Beijing, New Delhi, Montreal or Budapest. The same time and space that had 'slowed down' and narrowed for you when you were on the earth, paced up and widened when you were in the air.

What exist for us as small fragments of time and space is but a continuous 'now' for the One Who is watching everything from a timeless time, a spotless spot. Before His very eyes, John and Christina, Ramesh and Nina, Saleem and Zena are born, grownup, married, dead, buried and cremated. In His continuous span of 'now', Adolf Hitlers kill innocent people mercilessly in gas chambers and Lenins of the time enkindle Bolshevik Revolutions. The pomp and glory of Czars and Czarinas prosper and decay, civilisations are built and destroyed, nomadic tribes learn agriculture and city estates are established. He, in His indestructible perpetuity, watches the starving children of India and Africa and their leaders lost in corruption than wiping the tears of the millions. He, in His endless eternity, silently watches the construction of the Twin Towers at the same time as He watches it being terror-stricken on 26/11, the sufferings of the thousands, the tears of the millions. In His non-exhaustible 'now', He smiles when a Tajmahal of love is built in the sweet memories of a *khushkismet* Mumtaz and laments when a hundred stories of betrayals in love are written for petty worldly gains. Yet, detached and unbending in His resolve to interfere in the domain of free will that He so kindly bestowed upon mankind to make him His partner in love, the Great Being remains concealed in His eternal existence, in the words of a poet:

*O that liberated star of the eternity*
*Lost in his delight of tranquility!*

Our problem starts when we conceptualise God as something that is exclusive of us, a different, third entity. We think we are standing apart from God and weighing Him according to our own standards. The friend whom I've dedicated this book has been my greatest spiritual teacher in many ways. Once she related a wonderful metaphor about God and us. She told me a story about wheat cereals:

*The farmer used to weigh the wheat cereals and put them in the barn. One day, the cereals talked about the farmer and said: 'oh .. he weighs us everyday, can we weigh him today?'. My friend asked: 'Do you think the cereals can ever weigh the farmer who is himself holding the scale?' God is the same Farmer and we are tiny cereals in His barn. Which balance can we bring to weigh the Farmer? How can we weigh when He stands far away from our yards of measurement? Even the balance in which we will weigh Him is not ours but His!*

**Self-evident Brahma**

God is self-evident. It means we cannot prove Him without Him. Consider the Sun. Suppose, someone who has never seen the Sun, what the Sun is, what it looks like, how bright, how hot, etc.; what can you say to him? All the examples, similes and illustrations you might provide will fall far short of the reality of the Sun. If you tell him that the light of the Sun is brighter than that of a billion candles, still you are wrong and that person cannot guess the effulgence of the Sun. If you tell him that the Sun is a thousand times bigger than the earth, he will not understand because, as he never saw the Sun, he never saw the earth in its wholeness. But the moment the Sun rises, you can prove what the Sun is. The Sun is its own proof. God is His own proof. And, as in the metaphor of the farmer and the wheat cereals, everything is contained in God, including what we call time and space. We cannot measure God by time as time lives in Him not that He lives in time. We cannot imagine Him limited in a space because space is in Him not that He is in space. **All beginnings begin from Him, all ends end in Him.** How can, then, we poor creatures fathom the depth of beginning and scale the heights of the end of His creation!

Though the universe has its 'cycles' of evolution, and each cycle has a beginning and an end, it's impossible to reckon out the beginning and the end of the universe itself. For example, in Hinduism, they tell about the four epochs – *Sata Yug, Tretā Yug, Dwāpar Yug* and *Kali Yug* - each epoch marking a moral decline comparing to the previous epoch and, when the decline is on the climax, the Supreme Being winds up the entire existence, which is brought to 'naught', and from that 'nothingness' the Almighty creates everything anew. This '*Mahapralaya*' depicted in Hinduism is not different from what is called the Day of Judgement, Day of Resurrection or Qayamat referred to in Christianity and Islam.

Thus, all 'beginnings' and all 'ends' lie hidden in Him Who is the Originator and Destroyer of the entire appearance called creation.

**"I am the Alpha and the Omega, the Beginning and the End"**, said the Christ.

The 10th chapter of the Geeta elaborates the vast and mystic nature of God. Some of the attributes of God that Krishna refers to can be comprehended as follows:

*I'm enshrined as Soul in every being and I'm the Beginning, the Core and the End of every created object.*

(10:20)

*Ahmātmā gudākesha sarvabhuta āshaya sthitah;*
*Ahma ādishcha madhyam cha bhutānam unt yeva cha.*

*O Arjun! I'm the Beginning, the Core and the End of the creation.*

(10:32)

*Sargānām ādih antashcha madhyam chaiva Arjun.*

*I'm the all-destructive Death and the Cause of all that will come to pass.*

(10:34)

*Mrityuh sarva harshecha aham udbhavashcha bhavishyatām.*

And, ultimately, Krishna says to His disciple, Arjuna:

*O Arjuna! You need not know all the details. I am holding this entire universe just by a fraction of my 'yogamāyā', illimitable might. So, know only me as the essence.*

10:42

*Athavā bahunaitena kim gyātena tava Arjun;*
*Vishtabhyāham idam Kritsnameyankāshena sthito jagat.*

God, being the Primal Cause of all animate and inanimate worlds, is Himself with no beginning or end, like an eternal ocean with no visible shores. Like waves, like bubbles, the creation is born in Him and dies in Him moment by moment. So many times has this creation been made, destroyed and remade. This process of birth and death will continue and yet no birth is the first birth and no death is the last death.

**

8

# Love me so That I may Love Thee ..

*Even after all this time,*
*The Sun never says to the Earth:*
*'You owe me',*
*Look what happens with a love like that*
*It lights the whole sky.*

*— Hafez*

In the previous chapter, we discussed a particular point that of the *Karma* of the first man, argued by those who claim that they do not believe in previous existence. Another important question often raised with regard to 'previous birth' and 'reincarnation' in a 'bodily form' is this: **If one is born in this world as a consequence of his or her previous 'karma', it means he or she is brought in this world for some sort of punishment or reward. But then what is the use of the heaven and the hell? Does God have a 'double' system of reward and punishment?**

From a broad logical perspective, this world will not seem; to any conscientious observer of truth; a place substituted for heaven or hell. So, there is no question of double punishment or reward. Heaven and hell have their own business, this world has its own, and there can be no amalgamation.

As clarified in a previous chapter, though it is true that people are born in this world in the matrix of their respective '*karma*', it is not the Purpose of the creation. God created this universe to express His love and all He needs from us is our love for Him: love that's based on true understanding of our soul, its purpose and origin. The moment we know and feel that we are part of a Loving Self, the moment we become conscious that our soul has emanated from the Source that holds the key to its true delight, our soul aspires to set on a journey to meet that Best Beloved. However, if we are oblivious, careless to the reason of our birth and negligent to the soul's yearning for its Originator, we continue to live an ordinary life.

Baha'u'llah revealed the following short obligatory prayer that one must read daily. The importance of this prayer is that it reminds us of the purpose we are created for:

**I bear witness, O My God! That Thou hast created me to know Thee and to worship Thee. I testify at this moment to my powerlessness and to Thy might, to my poverty and to Thy wealth. There is none other God but Thee, the Help in peril, the Self-subsisting.**

**Love: The Prime Factor**

In the "**Hidden Words**", Baha'u'llah has uttered the purpose of human life in a clearer tone:

**O Son of Man! I loved thy creation, hence I created thee. Wherefore, do thou love Me, that I may name thy name and fill thy soul with the spirit of life.** (4)

**O Son of Being! Love Me, that I may love thee. If thou lovest Me not, My love can in no wise reach thee. Know this, O servant.** (5)

This whole universe is nothing but an expression of God's love. A Sufi poet *Mallika Muhammed Jāyasi* wrote:

**Oh, what's there but not hit by this arrow (of love)?**
**The whole universe is bearing its (sweet) pain.**
**These countless stars in the sky**
**Are but the arrows (of love) He shot.**

And it's not just a poetic imagination but a scientific truth that 'love', the power of attraction, gravitation, magnetic vibration, are the subatomic level energy systems that keep things together atom-by-atom. If this love, this power of attraction, will lose its balance, stars will fall asunder, planets will deviate from their paths, the oceans will surge, the mountains will split up and it will all look like the Day of Judgement, the annihilation!

The same 'annihilation' takes place everyday in every human being, nay, in every creature, when the love of God is forsaken. Lack of love for God produces Adolf Hitlers and Mussolinis, terrorists and extremists, rapists and perverts, and all sorts of violent, lunatic, unhinged and ungodly beings. All disturbances in individual and collective lives start when the gravitational pull between the Creator and the creation is imbalanced.

Unfortunately, however, the balance of this love cannot be meted out just by going to the church on the Sundays, offering '*namaz*' five times a day, nodding head in the temple at evening '*ārties*', arranging 'langars' at the gurudwārā, attending 19-day feast at the Baha'i House, or any other 'external' act without 'internal' motive. God is the Substance that can never be cheated by pretensions. That's why there are thousands upon thousands of churches, mosques and temples, and millions of people are attending them daily and yet life is so ugly, the soul is so unhappy. In lack of 'spiritual' love, 'religious' rituals are but insipid fruits.

Let's read that passage again:

**O Son of Being! Love Me, that I may love thee. If thou lovest Me not, My love can in no wise reach thee. Know this, O servant!**

Baha'u'llah does not say that "If thou lovest Me not, I will also not love thee". He says: "If thou lovest me not, My love can in no wise reach thee". The Sun is shedding its light 24 hours but if the earth turns her face, there is no sunlight in a hemisphere. The Sun is still giving its light to the earth and the other half is receiving it. If clouds cover the sunlight, it will not reach the earth in its full potential, but the Sun is still shedding its light. In the same way, God's love is constantly and continuously flowing towards us, even when we do not love Him. But, in that case, there is a covering, a cloudiness of 'ego' that does not let God's love penetrate our being. As a result, the internal chaos, the inner annihilation, the destruction 'within', the darkness pervading the soul, continues.

This is for what God created this universe: **To love Him**. He did not create us for any punishment. God has nothing to do with our '*karma*' good or bad, but He is concerned with our love. However, *karma* is the trail, the cycle, the vehicle, the route, the channel that brings us to this station of life. We chose the life we desired by expressing the God-gifted 'free will' through our deeds. Whom to blame?

And the same free will is still bestowed upon us, even in this new life we have inherited by our own choice. If things are not pleasing, if we really crave for a better life here or hereafter, the choice is still ours. The moment we stand with a resolute will to attract better things and better life, the clouds start dispersing, the darkness starts melting and love of God starts 'reaching' us. It was just standing outside our heart, bemoaning our condition, yearning and craving that we open the door and welcome this light.

**Angel and Satan**

It is a very significant thing that God bestowed 'free will' only on human beings. God created angels and angels are very good. They are not good because they chose to be good, but because God programmed them to be good. Angels have no choice to be bad. God created Iblis (the Satan) and cursed him to be evil. The Satan cannot choose to be good. And God created man and waxed proud, so much that He called out in joy 'come, see My wonderful creature'! Man is the only creature who can choose to be an angel and who can also choose to be a Satan. This excellence of the station of man is thus outlined in the Holy Quran:

> *"We have surely dignified Adam's progeny whom We hold on the land and the sea, and provided for them good things. We preferred them above many of those whom We created ..."*
>
> (Surah XVII : 70)

Had God wanted so, He could have 'forced' mankind to love Him. It was easy for Him! He could have 'forced' human beings to be essentially good and follow Him, but true love does not act that way. Would you like that the person whom you love so deeply, should love you back out of a compulsion? Would you like a lover who loves you unconsciously, without his or her active choice to love you? Such a 'forced' or 'programmed' lover may be a slave or a robot but not a 'lover' at all. Love is a fellowship, a feeling of being partners, a reciprocal understanding, an overwhelming emotion of heart between the two, a conscious choice to belong to someone! By giving us 'Free Will', God signed a permanent agreement of love with each one of us individually! We can choose to love Him, we can also choose not to love Him. He won't compel. Of course, He is craving for our love, waiting like an impatient lover that one day His beloved will return to Him, in His own clandestine ways trying to attract His lover by giving a myriad glimpse of His charming beauty in each atom of the creation, calling him in His tacit language from the valleys of tranquility and mounts of perceptions, beckoning him through shimmering stars and shivering blades of grasses, appearing before him in the most cherished face of his beloved to remind him of His aura and aurora, but under no condition does He 'force' His lover to woo Him. Everyone has to seek that Beloved by himself or herself and this is why we have free will, the power to choose.

**Eternal Hide and Seek**

In this eternal game of love, the Great Soul (*Paramātmā*) plays a Hide-and-Seek with the souls (*Atmā*) He created. In this 'spiritual hide-and-seek', He scatters all the souls in this vast cosmic labyrinth and He Himself sits in a place that is 'hidden from all' and, lo! How clever He is that He chose a place that is 'known to all'. At the same time, in this same game of hide-and-seek, He entangled a parallel hide-and-seek. Among the souls He scattered, He also scattered the soul mates of the souls. Each male and each female was given a 'soul mate' and now the game begins! Each individual soul has to find his or her soul mate. God has enabled every soul to identify his or her soul mate by recognising the images of his or her own soul in the soul mate:

**Love! I heard in this great universe**
**Souls were made, then sent dispersed**
**Then ... on each soul God embossed**
**A faint image of his soul-mate flossed**

There is only one soul mate for each soul and there

is only one Beloved of all. And until and unless the soul has eventually found its soul mate, and the Best Beloved, there is no rest, no peace, and no end to this 'hide-and-seek', even if it takes a trillion years of the journey of the soul, even if a million times one has to be born and die.

The task seems challenging, but not for the one who understood this Sufi philosophy of a poet who **saw the 'Noor-e-Khodā' (the light of God) in the 'purdāh' (veil) of the 'husn-e-butān' (the beauty of the idol)**. The beauty of God is veiled in the beauty of this world. The love for God has no contradiction with love for His creatures. The true love that reflects itself in the passionate feelings for the fiancé or the fiancée, in our deep longings to find him or her even if this life becomes a ransom, in ardent hopes and pure desires, in fervent emotions to bestow all happiness on the beloved even if the sky is to be ransacked, in the divine feelings of forgiveness and tolerance for the loved one even when everything goes wrong. All these are only some of the attributes that God reflects in His love for us. The same attributes are the criteria of true love between a soul and its soul mate, a man and a woman, and, also between a soul and God. Thus, our 'mortal' love, when held in the true spirit of love, shows us the path of 'immortal' love. Nobody can reach the destination of Immortal Love without passing through the landmark of the mortal love.

It is mere foolishness to think and preach that love for God is different from this mortal plane and can only be achieved by ascetics and saints. Those who follow the path of rigorous practice, refrain from the shadow of mortal beauty so that their soul is not sullied, those who meditate and strive to see the Supreme Beloved in their inner beings while the entire world is asleep, are endeavouring to find the same 'Object' by an arduous labour as the lover finds in the sweet embrace of his or her beloved.

> *We had not known that we loved God, hardly it may be that we believed in Him; yet looking backward upon our life we discover, in our exploration of the pathways of woods, in our delight in the lonely places of hills, in that mysterious claim that we have made, unavailingly on the woman that we have loved, the emotion that created this insidious sweetness.*
>
> (W.B. Yeats, in Introduction to Tagore's *Geetānjali*)

**The Way to the Best Beloved**

We are here in a world where flowers bloom, rivers warble, birds sing, and bees hum. Love is the intrinsic force here. How can we remain untouched? Where will we escape? So why not welcome it? But how? What is love? Is love there in the flesh? Does love reside in hugs and kisses, touches of warmth and desires of physical union? This physical body is the emerging point of love because a form is needed for love's birth. However, once born on the physical plane, love denies the limits of bodies. Once the fledgling of love is born out of the shell of the 'body', it strives to soar high in the realm of the 'soul'. And there it finds the Best Beloved.

The one who found his or her soul mate is close to finding the Best Beloved. Love that we enjoy in this world becomes a divine tunnel through which we pass, unknowingly though, and suddenly find that the beloved is lost. The one on whom we centred all our hopes vanished in the mist of death and nothingness. The one who had become our universe, left us in lurch where we stand broken and bewildered. Those pledges of eternal companionship, those cherished desires of two souls to walk hand-in-hand in the moonlit night dissolve in the naught of oblivion, because this is the destiny of the earthly love. With benumbed senses, with lost hopes, with broken wings of desires, and with a soul scarred to its core, we look haplessly for a beam of light which can bring back the charming face of the beloved. But mortal beloveds are lost in mortal mires. Between these two souls there was a barrier ... this body ... and bodies are not to last forever! In those dismal hours, from that pang of love for the beloved, a new love is born, a new hope glimmers on that end of the tunnel. When all have left, even our self has left our self, the Best Beloved appears! And now body is not a barrier!

If human love becomes a bond of spiritual depth and true understanding of two souls, God remains no longer hidden, because the place He chose 'hidden from all' is the place 'known to all', our heart, where every beloved lives.

So, this is why God created us, to love Him, to seek Him, to find Him, to reach Him – and do all this by our own volition and not by force!

This world is a place where all souls are scattered, all soul mates are dispersed and where God, too, is hiding in our 'core'. In this labyrinthine quest of love, whether it is love for our true soul mate or for that Best Beloved, many angels and fairies appear to guide us to the 'Hiding Place' of our Beloved. These angels and fairies are none but our own purity and eagerness. And in this labyrinthine quest of love, whether it is love for our true soul mate or for that Best Beloved, many Satans and devils also appear to drive us away from the straight path of love. Greed for temporary satisfaction at the cost of heavenly gain, faithlessness and defilement, are some of these Satans and devils.

This material world is that very place where the 'muscles' of our 'free will' are tested and challenged to make them stronger for our further flight to a higher realm, alas many of us tend to fail this test by giving up to knick-knacks.

**Our Selection and Free Will**

This world, as Prophet Zoroaster pointed out hundreds of years ago, is a battlefield of the divine Ahura Mazda who wants to lead us to light, and the crooked Ahriman binding us to an endless darkness. We have to decide which way to go.

This world is that Mega Market which heaps before us a rich and mixed collection of 'commodities', some of them so dazzling that they can 'blind' our soul, and some of them fading like the pupils of my bed-ridden Mom but, yet, the assets of my love!

This world is a long corridor with many a phantom passing through the aisle, fascinating and inviting, and there is my beloved at the end of the corridor, silently waiting for me.

It is on me to hold the hands of that fascinating charmer who is whatever but not my soul mate, and it is on me to pass by quietly and reach my serene-faced fairy to tell her, "O My Love! See, so many charmers posed to spellbind me, but I rushed to hug you, My Beloved!" And then feel her soul-touching kisses on my lips and her whispers in my ear: "I'm proud of you, O Dearest!"

It is my choice to buy the 'commodities' of sensual flights and spiritual abasements. It is my choice to buy the 'commodities' my soul can easily carry and fly with.

I am responsible to listen to the wicked suggestions of the devils of greed and glamour, of barters and betrayals, of wizardries and witchcrafts; and I am also free to dive deep into my pure subconscious to listen to the whispers of the angels and fairies smiling at me and pointing to that lonesome but straight road to love and peace.

Whatever course I choose as John or Christina, Ramesh or Nina, Saleem or Zena, will not only decide my meeting with the Beloved but also my next life.

In all these selections I will be making in this world, it would be so important for me to remember that this life is a preparation for that life. This world is a replica of that world. This earth is reflection of the sky. What I choose here, I choose for hereafter. What I act here, for that I send a reaction in that world.

*"Assuredly, I say to you, whatever you bind on earth will be bound in heaven, and whatever you loose on earth will be loosed in heaven".*

(The Bible, Matthew 18:18)

It is chocked in Quran:

*"Whosoever is blind here will be blind hereafter, and further from the road."*

(The Quran, XVII: 72)

# 9

# I 'Attracted' This Life

*Explore the River of the Soul;*
*whence or in what order you have come.*
*— Zoroaster*

A major discovery in the 19th century, in the realities of the physical world, was of the 'Law of Attraction'. Though people knew about the existence of such a law even before, but a new scientific approach gave it a widespread recognition. The discovery of the fact that what we call or perceive as 'matter' is nothing but a compact mass of energy with different vibrations and magnetic coherence completely changed the paradigm of viewing this physical world. Nothing exists in solid form as we see them, but in the form of highly charged energy packets that attract similar energies and build up into matter.

### Opposites

When the scientists were talking about these 'vibrations' and believing that the entire universe is but a space where these vibrating energies are moving freely and rapidly, a scientist named **Paul Dirac** in 1928 posed a challenging question that changed our perception about matter. Paul believed that as everything has a conforming opposite in this universe – action and reaction, day and night, love and hatred, vice and virtue - even 'matter' must have an 'antimatter', electron must have anti-electron (which he termed as 'positron') and so on. Just four years later, in 1932, another scientist, **Carl D. Anderson**, discovered positron. Paul Dirac stirred us to think that if everything is 'vibrating' and 'moving', there must be something that is 'fix' and 'static' in this fleeting and changing world. It is that fix and static 'antimatter' which provides space for everything to vibrate because nothing can move or vibrate without space.

That static element is 'consciousness' which is not a matter but an antimatter; not worldly but divine. That consciousness is in the form of thought, even in such things as we term as inanimate.

This is the greatest discovery of science till date which signifies the presence of a 'spiritual entity' behind every atom. In Hindu spiritualism, **Vishnu** is considered to be one of the 'Trinity' and is responsible for the preservation of the universe. The very word 'Vishnu' (Vi: + Anu) means 'the one who is systematically (vi:) present in every atom (anu)'. Now we truly know that Vishnu lives in every atom in the form of a non-atom, in every matter as a non-matter, and that is how everything is preserved in the universe. Now, you call it 'Vishnu' or call it 'consciousnesses – what's the difference?

Once we know that everything is 'consciousness' – comprised of 'thought' – it is easy to understand that every reality in this physical world is but a vibrational outcome of thought. **In the beginning was the Word and the Word was with God**. **"Aham Brahmāsmi"** (I am the Brahma, the Creator) – this thought gave birth to this universe. Since **God created man in His own image**, the power of conscious thought became a natural legacy to mankind. **What a man thinks, so he is**.

**Similarities**

The "Law of Attraction", as it is termed today, is nothing different from the "Law of *Karma*" – the Law of Cause and Effect. Newton's third law - **For every action, there is an equal and opposite reaction** – also has the same purport. Each thought is a cause, each result is an effect. Nothing can escape this endless circle. There can be no result without an action and there can be no action failing to bring an effect. This is the law of attraction. As such, good thoughts beget good results, bad thoughts beget bad results, and no thoughts beget no results.

Our present life on this planet is a consequence, an effect, and the cause is '**our desire to be born**'. Had we not desired to be born on this planet, with such and such capacities, so and so atmosphere, we were not going to be born as such. Therefore, each individual - John and Christina, Ramesh and Nina, Saleem and Zena – is himself or herself responsible for being where he or she is on this plane of existence.

There is a Law of Attraction working through our free will all the time. However, many modern protagonists of the Law of Attraction believe that LOA is working only in our current life. We are whatever we thought. Our present is a reflection of our past and our future will be exactly what we continuously think today. Of course, it is true but 'Past' and 'Future' go far beyond this life. The main premise of the Law of Attraction, as put in the famous movie - **THE SECRET**, is 'Thoughts become Things'. But if the Law of Attraction is working only in the present realm of life, many things will remain unanswered. For example, in this world a 6 month old child is raped and misused, and even killed. Now, a six month old child is not so mature and experienced that he or she will 'deliberately' think and attract rape and murder. So ... if "thoughts become things", we must admit that some 'thoughts' which became 'things' in this life must have had their root in our past lives. Or else, the Law of Attraction is a nonsense fuss!

If we consider the Law of Attraction having its effect only in this life, one cannot even give a satisfactory answer as to why so many generations of mankind suffered slavery? Who attracted to be massacred by the hands of Saddam Hussains and Neroes of their times? Why natural disasters kill so many people? Why a train or a plane accident takes place? Why wars break among nations? It is not possible that thousands of people collectively 'attracted' a holocaust! It will be a blunt foolishness to say that those hundreds and thousands of people willingly attracted their murder and slavery, injustice and ruin. These blatant truths only refer to the fact that whatever is reflected now in our individual or collective life is not just a consequence of 'one' present life but 'many' previous lives. It also suggests that there is a Destiny for this world and it is not always controlled by our own free will.

**Accumulations**

Desires are those propelling forces or 'wings' to our souls that drive our being to the next stage of life and decide the environment, people and places that we aspired to associate with. When we die, the body decays but the 'consciousness' (the soul) is free from decay. It soars to the 'next steps of life' with all its attributes earned on its earthly life, with all the impacts and impressions deeply imbibed. If a person loved someone very deeply in the previous life, he or she travels to the next step of consciousness where the impressions of the previous love are automatically acquired. It is exactly like the features of parents automatically acquired by children through a genetic coding system so intelligently designed by Nature. Each desire (means strong desire and not just 'wishes') is carried forward in a 'coded' way and as the individual is born again, these 'codes' are deciphered by the soul to bring the things, people and situations that the person had decided to attract in his or her life. Simply put, every desire is an indestructible energy-pattern which builds upon itself, gaining strength from its previous stimulus and moving forward from that pre-secured pitch.

Arjuna, the devoted disciple of Krishna, asked Him about the consequences in case of a person who did his best to tread on the path of 'yoga' (unity with self and/or God), practised self-control, but deviated in the end. What is his destiny?

What will happen of him who was good and virtuous throughout his life but slipped ultimately? Will all his efforts on the path of virtue come to nothingness? If so, how pitiful is his condition that he did not reap the benefits of goodness just because of a failure in the end! What will happen of him who maintained a sane and sober life except when, in a weak moment, he succumbed to a sinful temptation? Will all his sanity and sobriety be of no avail because of a last moment aberration? What will happen of him who loved his fiancée so dearly throughout his life that he was ready to bring the skyflower for her, alas she left him for some other greed! All those years of his dedicated love to that lady will end because she chose to betray? If such is the case in this universe, nobody will care for a 'process', but for an 'end result'. Nobody will dare to do anything good because he might fail in the end.

Responding to this basic query in the realm of action, God gives an eternal surety through Krishna:

> *"O Arjuna! Such a person is destroyed neither in this world nor hereafter, because he who performs good acts will never see his downfall. The one who fell from the path of 'yoga', goes to heavenly realms and after a prolonged stay in those realms, he is born in the house of a noble and virtuous person or, he is born in the lineage of learned 'yogis', a rare birth indeed. There, in that new existence, he automatically regains the accumulated virtues of his previous life which stir him to stronger endeavours for perfection. By*

*the merits of his previous life, he is – by default – drawn towards God"*

(summarised from 'Geetā', Chapter 6:40-44)

**Justice**

So, no effort is frustrated, no desire is sent to oblivion. If we have been good throughout our life, we will attract further goodness, no matter if we failed a little. If we lived a chaste and pious life, we will continue to live so in the next birth, after a process of purgation on account of being succumbed to a short sinful temptation. And if we loved someone from the depth of our heart, we will find him or her in the next life, even if we have been cheated in this momentary life. In this life, whatever we stuck ourselves to will stick to us in the next life – good as good, evil as evil; love as love, hatred as hatred; faith as faith, betrayal as betrayal; plenty as plenty, lack as lack.

*For whoever has, to him more will be given, and he will have abundance, but whoever does not have, even what he has will be taken away from him.*

(The Bible, Matthew 13:12)

The law of attraction is, again, a vital proof how God gave us the absolute power of free will.

An important thing to remember, under the law of attraction (or the law of *karma*) is that this law, as any other law of God, is inanimate and it cannot choose between right and wrong. For example, if something is falling towards the earth, accidentally or purposely, the law of gravity cannot 'decide' if it should attract the object or not. It will work in both cases. Fire burns. It cannot 'choose' not to burn the house of an innocent person. The magnet attracts whether we keep the iron near the magnet knowingly or unknowingly.

In the same way, the law of attraction (or the law of *karma*) is not concerned if we attracted something in our life intentionally or unintentionally. Whatever came in the ambit of our 'strong desire' – positive or negative – was drawn to us and took shape in the world of reality. This is like a bullet or an arrow shot, and its hitting a human. Whether we shot the bullet or arrow purposely or accidentally does not make any difference 'in the eyes of the law' and we cannot escape punishment.

Many times in our lives we pay too much attention on 'unwanted' things and give them a copious room in the ambit of our 'strong desires' – things that we would have never wanted in our life, and yet we unconsciously chose them by making them the centre of our hatred, envy, fear, doubt, repulsion and so many negative emotions. We did not like a certain man or woman, we hated to live in a certain atmosphere, we envied the other being so rich, we doubted the love that made our life a heaven, we despised the person who could be an asset to our business – and, in this way, all these things that we did not want became a part of our 'desire energy system', through negative focus, and **we attracted the very things we did not want to attract**. We attracted a consort we never loved, a city we never liked, an office where all are inimical, sounds that are unpleasing, auras that are abhorring, things that are disgusting, life that is far away from being our bliss! Hope this answers the query of those who complaint and say that 'I had not desired this life, these people, this workplace, this atmosphere. Yet, how did I get them?'

All great religions have advised mankind to focus on positive aspects. This popular prayer revealed in the **Brihadaranyaka Upanishad** invites us for the same:

**Lead me from falsehood to truth!**
**Lead me from darkness to light!**
**Lead me from death to immortality!**

And this journey from 'negative' to 'positive' mindset must start from within; not just outwardly but inwardly, because even if we outwardly focus on good things but in our subconscious we are still hatching the old rotten eggs of negative feelings, our life will not change. To change our circumstances outside, we must change our feelings inside, because unless we change our heart, even God cannot change our condition:

*Allah does not change His grace that He bestowed upon people until they first change what their hearts contain.*

(The Quran, VIII:53)

When the Christ asked us **"to turn the other cheek to whoever slaps"**, He was not teaching us to be a coward, nor that we should not be self-defensive, but simply that we should not let a revengeful thought keep gnawing us inside and harm our soul with its erosive impact. Thus, the good virtues that all religions teach – kindness, truthfulness, obedience, forgiveness, generosity (and you can add many more) – should not just be taken as 'dry religious teachings' but as vital prescriptions for life.

To conclude, we are born in this world because we chose to do so. Since beginning, our existence has been nothing but an unfolding expression of our own desires and it will continue to be so. It is a progressive journey of a soul in the ocean of eternity and each progress has gained its strength from the previous cycle of existence. This being the fact, it is very true to say, as the poet, **William Earnest Henley**, said:

**I am the master of my fate.**
**I am the captain of my soul.**

### Accumulated Effect

This being the truth, I can decide my future life. I can decide who will be my companions, in which surroundings I want to live, which country, which society and under plentiful or a constrained resources of life. I can even choose not to be born again in this ephemeral universe where people and things come and go and leave us bewildered one day.

This being the truth, it is clear that I do not need to be dismayed by my sufferings and afflictions in this world as rich rewards are waiting for me in the next world. At the same time, I must not wax vainglorious in this transient life for my power or pelf, for what I have gained now is nothing but a result of my labours in so many past lives.

Most of us know about 'Dhruva', a child whose story is found in Hindu Puranic scriptures. It needs to be retold here in brief in this unique context. Dhruva was son of a king named Uttānapāda who had two queens, and Dhruva was from his elder queen. The king loved the younger queen and her child more than the elder queen and her son Dhruva who never enjoyed his father's love and his heart was in deep pains. His mother told him, in order to console, that he should not worry too much if his worldly father does not love him because his Heavenly Father, God, always loves him. It was a great solace for the child and he believed in what his mother said. Faith is truly a powerful thing! Dhruva's faith in Heavenly Father was so profound that He really appeared before him to hug him and embrace him. He enjoyed the company of God for long and grew into an elder boy. Then one day, a feeling of pride and vainglory sneaked in his mind as he thought that God lives with him, eats with him, plays with him, the same God whom no one can perhaps meet in this mortal life! Knowing his thought, God asked him to go into the forest and fetch a glass of water for Him from a fountain as He felt thirsty. Dhruva wandered deep into the forest but found no fountain of water. However, he happened to see a big mountain far away, a mountain made of bones and skeletons. It seemed that millions of sages, yogis and seers had spent their lives on that mountain - standing and sitting in postures of prayers, yoga and meditation and they had died there!

Dhruva rushed back to God and expressed his pity for those who could not unite with Him though they practised such austerities. **"These are your skeletons, Dhruva!"**, said God, **"in millions of your previous births you aspired for Me, wanted union with Me, craved to see Me in this Form. A million times were**

**you born and you died but not until this life were you meritorious enough to find Me!"**

Many of us are not different from Dhruva. We think that we have earned these riches by virtue of our own sweat and labour, we think it is we who have all these wonderful achievements in life, we mock at those who fail in their endeavours, we exalt ourselves over the other who lag behind us in this race of life. We forget that what we have achieved today is not ours just by a single effort, many lives we spent, many times we slipped and failed.

Our belief in the 'self-responsibility' in choosing this life also frees us from a mindset of dissatisfaction and blaming others. This belief guarantees that we are not living in a world which began with our birth on this planet and ends with our death on this earth, but in a world which is eternal and everlasting. There are many good acts one performs in this life but was seldom rewarded, and there are also many sinful acts one performs here for which he was never punished. **But in the Final Judgement nobody escapes.**

> *The Hour is surely coming. But I will keep it hidden so that every soul is rewarded for what it endeavoured to achieve.*
>
> (The Quran, XX: 15)

Our belief in exercising our 'free will' to be born as we are born now, also implies that whatever wrong has been done to us is because we might have wronged someone else, and whatever good has been done to us is also because we might have done good to someone else. As such, we need not wail or weep but learn a lesson that we will not use our life in harming others and thus harming ourselves. Each of us must accept his or her own responsibility for his or her acts. Whatsoever I will do unto the other would be done unto me, in this life or that life, I just can't escape.

There are many "modern" thinkers whose fashion is to bask in the sunlight of so-called 'logical' understanding of things, and for them the Law of Attraction or the Law of *Karma* has nothing to do with right or wrong, vice or virtue, good or bad, moral or immoral. They just explain everything in the light of cause and effect. Of course, everything is 'cause and effect', but good causes have good outcomes (rewards) and bad causes have bad outcomes (punishments). When Adam and Eve were 'thrown out' of the Garden of Eden, it was not God Who pulled them by their arms and threw them down on the earth. It was their act of disobedience to God (a bad cause) which resulted in their self-expulsion from heaven (a punishment). We are not living in a 'neutral' world which is not concerned with choices we make. Rather, we are living in a world whose sole purpose is to teach us how to make spiritual choices over material choices, and until we've exactly mastered this art, our soul cannot escape being bound with a body. There is no Law of the universe which does not carry a spiritual significance, no world of God that does not mirror forth the qualities of the Divine Kingdom, no journey of the soul that is not a spiritual journey.

**

# 10

# Levels of Consciousness

*All are but parts of one stupendous whole*
*Whose body is Nature and God the soul.*

*— Alexander Pope*

God is the Creator who Fashioned this entire universe which is in a continuous process of birth and death, creation and destruction, evolution and annihilation and growth too. This earth that we inhabit was not the same always. As the scientists say, it was nothing but a hot molten rock in the beginning, then water emerged, it cooled down and gradually the atmosphere was created. Only then the living beings came into existence.

Charles Darwin (1809-1882) gave his popular **Theory of Evolution** to prove that in this continuous unfold-ment of life-pattern on the earth, all beings descended from an original species. Darwin also drew out a very terrible picture of life in which there is a "*struggle for survival*" going on continuously because these "animals" (including men) are producing children more than available resources. As a result, those who are "*the fittest*" overcome their rivals as they succeed in adapting themselves best to their environment. Even though Darwin agreed that man has 'noble qualities', 'sympathy', 'benevolence', and 'God-like intellect', he was adamant in his belief that "*man still bears in his bodily frame the indelible stamp of his lowly origin*".

It was naturally difficult for such a pessimistic scientist, plunged in the 'lowly origin', to believe that any 'omnipotent God would have designedly created parasitic wasps with the express intention of their feeding within the living bodies of Caterpillars.'

The whole theory of Charles Darwin is based on the lopsided view of 'survival' in the same way as the entire theory of Sigmund Freud in the area of human psychology is inspired by the stimulus of 'sex'. For Sigmund Freud, man had no other desire than those rooted in sex, and for Darwin this whole spiritual creation of God is but a poor 'live or die' battle.

Darwinism has already met its defeat in modern times. The two broad bases on which Darwinian Evolution falls flat are these:

1. If it is true that in millions of years certain 'apes' evolved into 'human beings', why no more 'apes' are evolving into men? Why the cycle stopped? Moreover, if man is an evolution from 'ape', there must have been different phases of transformation or transmutation in this gradual evolution. That is, there must be many 'editions' of 'ape-man' creatures in between. The same

'intermediary editions' must exist for other animals that evolved from their ancestors. Where are these 'intermediary editions' such as, to say, half lizard-half crocodile, half man-half gorilla, half snake-half fish, and so on?

2. If 'survival' is the only reason for this rat-race or this neck-slitting competition of life, how do Evolutionists define the feelings of 'love' and 'sympathy', 'benevolence' and 'noble qualities' that Darwin has himself attested as qualities of human beings? What these 'God-like intellects' have to do in the 'survival' process? For example, if there is only one piece of bread, the mother should eat that loaf of broad herself rather than sparing it for her child and choose death or discomfort for herself. Lovers should not sacrifice their lives in love and people should not die for great causes. If 'survival of the fittest' is the governing principle of the creation, the whole earth is destined to go in the hands of despotic rulers who will exploit the resources of the earth for their own survival. In a world with such a blind 'natural selection', Tagores and Gandhis, Lincolns and Martin Luther Kings, Tolstoys and Gorkis, Picassos and Bachs, Socrates and Laotses will surely be the most 'unfit' citizens. And, in such an amphitheatre of bull-fighting, there will be no room for Abraham and Moses, Krishna and Buddha, Christ and Mohammad, Mahavir and Nanak, Bab and Baha'u'llah.

No doubt, we are living in a world continuously expanding its capacities, developing its life-expressive abilities and evolving its individual and institutional framework, it must be remembered that 'evolution' takes place in homogeny of one's own kind. It is not a heterogeneous concept. As such, everything evolves in its own sphere and not in the sphere of other objects.

**Abdu'l-Baha**, the Appointed Expounder of the teachings of Baha'u'llah, has clearly stated that just because of this finding of science that mankind appeared on the earth after the animals, it will be erroneous to believe that man evolved from animals:

**Animal having preceded man is not a proof of the evolution, change and alteration of the species, nor that man was raised from the animal world to the human world.** – Some Answered Questions

No 'being' ever evolved into other 'being'. The Almighty God has exclusively created, since beginning, the five levels of 'consciousness' and they are: Mineral Kingdom, Vegetable Kingdom, Animal Kingdom, Human Kingdom, and the Holy Spirit. Though it is true that an evolution takes place for each individual and even for this entire universe, it is not the evolution as described by Darwin.

**Physical and Spiritual**

This evolution takes place in the spiritual perspective of a soul, and not in the physical perspective of the body. The Quran says that Allah created man from a lump of clay. It is true in its deep significance that when God infuses soul in a human being, it is first in its primal mineral state like clay. All the attributes of God are 'inscribed' upon this soul in the same way as all limbs and organs are given to a foetus in the womb. But they are not developed exactly as the physical and mental faculties of a foetus are undeveloped. When a child is born in this world, it is not only an opportunity and facility for the growth of its physical attributes but also the attributes of its soul. Physical capacities are developed by the use of free will of the individual as well as strains, tests and trials imposed by Nature. When a kid starts to walk, he falls many times and many times his knees are scratched, elbows bruised. But these tests and trials from Nature, together with the natural urge to exercise his willpower, eventually helps him walk on this hard surface. So is with soul. God puts many tests and trials before a soul through which it comes to realise its hidden potentialities and its purpose. With these hard-won experiences, man 'chooses' the attributes that will help his soul to ascend to a further station.

Then the soul, from its 'near-inert' (ignorant) state, attains the station like vegetables. It aspires to grow towards the light of Truth still the 'inertia' acquired from the initial stage binds it to earthly chains. This aspiration, however, lifts it further to its 'animalistic' status. It acquires more freedom and movement to act in noble ways. It has more expressive consciousness, intuition and voluntary patterns. Then it attains a further stage of the soul's journey when it learns to behave like 'humans'.

A soul does not become human just because the soul is reflected in a human body. Many souls are still in their mineral stage. They are people who behave like Timur Lenk. What else can be said? There is a story about Timur. Once he was passing through a forest with his band of army. A poor shepherd woman was crying and lamenting near a ditch. Timur asked: "Why are you crying?" She pointed to the ditch and said that her child fell in the ditch and she couldn't bring him out. Timur said, "Wait a minute!" He held his spear tightly, stabbed it into the chest of the screaming child and pulled him out. Is such a soul not in 'mineral' state? Even minerals are better, because brooks of water spring from stones but a small dew of mercy does not shine in these Timur Lenks who are found in all countries and in all times. They rape children, they burn houses in the name of religion, they murder the strangers for a dime or a penny, they oust their old parents on roads in a chilly winter night, and they do every possible act to deface this beautiful face of life created by God so tenderly and carefully.

**Graded Consciousness**

A soul does not become human just because it reflects in the human body. There are people who captivated their own daughters in a cell and exploited her lifelong. There are people who killed their own brothers, even parents and children. There are 'human beings' who raped and butchered children in their puberty and dumped their skeletons in the drains of their house. Can animals ever be worse than them? Those who proudly say that humans are superior to animals are inebriated fools. This is another 'fostered lie' like a similar 'fostered lie' that 'women are inferior to men'. Animals never rape their young ones. They do not kill other animals randomly. They do not exploit their youngsters as 'child labours'. They do not go and judge other people on the basis of their race, religion, caste, creed, love affairs, marital status, wealth or colour.

Since time immemorial, these five levels of consciousness remained in their own respective realms and will never step out of their 'kingdom'. There can be improvement in their individual spheres. For example, natural and human factors can cause the formation of 'developed' minerals, more sophisticated metals, but no mineral can ever evolve into a plant.

Though the **Mineral Kingdom**, the first level of consciousness, seems 'lifeless' to us, we must remember that some hundreds years ago even plants were considered inanimate, till Sir J.C. Bose made his experiments to show they have life.

As we discussed in a previous chapter, everything in this world has a counterpart or an 'opposite'. Every meaning and movement in life is possible because of these 'two opposites'. We understand 'life' in the light of 'death' and 'death' in the light of 'life'. We know 'love' from 'no love' and 'no love' from 'love'. 'Day' is known because 'night' exists, and without 'black' there is no identity of 'white'. At the same time, we understand in life that there is a 'fine thread', a very 'subtle difference', a very 'thin and filmy wall' that differentiates between these two 'opposites' of life. Just by one breathing life stands apart from death; between 'love' and 'no love' often a small reason becomes decisive; small tints of grey decide between 'black' and 'white'; and slowly the 'day' merges into 'night'. Amidst evident lifelessness, life exists in the same manner. In every 'seemingly unconscious' object, consciousness is found in the same way.

When there is 'matter', there must also be 'spirit', and now it is well-proven that what we call matter is, in its root, a living consciousness. We are not living in a 'dead' universe but a universe in which every atom is alive – vibrant, harmonious and ready to serve the purpose designated to it by the Creator. However, we cannot easily discover this 'consciousness' in the mineral kingdom because it is subtle.

The second level of consciousness is **Vegetable Kingdom**. In plants, we can see a more expressive level of consciousness, enriched with colours, smell, growth, reproduction, breathing and food cycle. They are imbued with more life and vitality than minerals but, like minerals, they also cannot move or change their place. Again, though it is possible to produce better 'breeds' of plants and flowers, more productive species of tomato and cabbage, plants cannot evolve into animals.

**Animal Kingdom** is on the third level of consciousness. Animals have all the qualities of the previous two levels, minerals and plants, but they possess a loftier degree of consciousness with capability to move and respond to Nature and environment in a systematic and communicative way. They have 'instincts' to guide them and 'common sense' to know the things around. Efforts have been made since beginning of the human history to tame some of the animals and use their services in agriculture and other spheres of activities. Horses, donkeys, mules, monkeys, camels, hares, turtles, snakes, crocodiles, dolphins, elephants, cows, buffaloes and so many other animals have lived in the company of men for thousands of years. Though man was able to train them efficiently to carry on various tasks, no animal has ever acquired any human qualities for building houses, wearing nice clothes, using internet, visiting malls and cafes, reading books, or composing music or poesy. Because animals are not possessive of 'free will' as humans are and even if a billion year will have elapsed, no 'monkey' can evolve into 'man'.

The **Human Kingdom** is stationed on the next level of consciousness where it possesses all the qualities of the mineral, vegetable and animal kingdoms, but it has an added attribute, Free Will. Human mind is capable of innovating new things and 'choose' what to do, what not to. On the other hand, birds and animals, insects and crawlers have always lived in a 'fixed' style as prescribed by the nature, because they cannot 'choose' to act differently. In every sphere of action, only man has 'freedom' to decide the course while all other beings act as guided by nature only.

On the apex of the layers of consciousness, we find the **Holy Spirits**. All the Messengers of God stand on this level. They have all the qualities of mankind, and that is why all the Messengers were underestimated and disrespected in their lifetime as ordinary human beings, but they have some added attributes, including the Faith of God and Infallibility. This "Faith" is the reason that lifts them above mankind, and this "Infallibility" is a direct authority from God that frees them from errors. They represent on this earth: the wisdom and knowledge, foresight and providence of God, so that they can guide the mankind towards the horizon of Truth.

No human being, however great and intelligent and versed in arts and sciences, can ever achieve these qualities and hence no 'man' can ever evolve into a 'Messenger' or an 'angel'.

We have already witnessed in the progressive development of human civilisation that great men of accomplishments; artists, scientists, poets, philosophers, sages and seers, leaders, reformers, thinkers and religious leaders; have emerged from time to time and have greatly contributed to the development of human society. Their ideas spurred human minds. At the same time, we also know that however perfect they were in their time, their inefficacy was soon to be proved.

Karl Marx, for example, was a remarkable social protagonist of his time and his ideas helped in changing the fate of the labour class all over the world. Yet, Marxism soon lost its significance and the social system based on his theology is no longer a popular doctrine of our time. Charles Darwin was a great scientist who turned the direction of human thought but the Theory of Evolution was soon refuted. Einstein, though a celebrity of his time, is now enveloped in a mist of doubts as further developments in science have outdated some of his observations. Many old beliefs and theories in sciences and arts, philosophies and psychologies, medicines and humanities have been rejected in course of time though they were propounded by highly intelligent scholars.

On the other hand, the spiritual teachings of Abraham, Moses, Zoroaster, Krishna, Buddha, Christ, Mohammad, Bab, Baha'u'llah (and all other great Messengers) stand right on the touchstone of time and are still guiding the mankind. We see two scientists, two artists, two leaders, two scholars, confronting each other on a burning issue and often having no unanimity, but have ever two Messengers confronted each other? That is because they all proclaim the same inviolable truth. Krishna did not lay a moral precept that is not justified by Jesus Christ. Mohammad did not utter any spiritual truth that Baha'u'llah had to contradict. All Messengers are Infallible. They cannot fail, they cannot err, and they cannot deviate from what is Truth.

Therefore, there is nothing like 'Darwinian Evolution'. Man was always man, monkey was always monkey.

> *Man is soul, not body. Though physically man belongs to the animal kingdom, his soul lifts him above the rest of creation.*
>
> (Abdu'l-Baha in Paris Talks.)

Since man is the only creation imbued with 'Free Will', he is the only creation with desire, and hence, he is the only creation to transform his desires into Action or Karma. Therefore, it will be fallacious to believe, as often quoted by Hindus, that one attains his birth as a human being after passing through a cycle of 8400000 'Yonis' (species). Believing in this means, for example, if I was a cat in the last birth, I did something good to be born into human being in this life. But what good can a cat do when she can't even 'think' beyond an intuitive pattern? No animal can do good or bad. No other beings but humans can initiate 'karma'. So there is no question that I was a horse or a rat or a stone or a cauliflower in my last birth, nor is there even a blind possibility that I will be born into a pig or a zebra, a caterpillar or a butterfly, a fern or pumice in my next life. All I was and will be is something like John or Christina, Ramesh or Nina, Saleem or Zena ....

**

# Death: The Messenger of Joy

My dreams are endless, I've countless desires
They'll reveal themselves in a thousand attires
My bones and flesh will return to earth
But my soul will rejoice in eternal mirth.

When I was a child in Darbhanga, my lovely adolescent city, we had a small group of children who had just learnt swimming in one of the big pools near my house. Our summertime fun mostly included swimming in that pool and playing water sports, especially our favourite '*Dive and Seek*' in which 5-6 children would dive under water and try to catch each other. The pool was too big and yet all of us were very versed swimmers, diving in the water and emerging some 50-60 metres away. It was an exciting game! Diving was something like 'hiding' our existence for some seconds and soon, oh, lo! the heads surfaced!

Today when I am such a grownup child in my 40's, that '*Dive and Seek*' of the teenage days whispers out a new meaning to my soul. This has become a symbolic game in the pool of existence where life and death, like two children of God, merrily play together. Death dives, life seeks. 'Diving' appears like 'disappearance', but still there is existence underneath that will surface its head soon! Death looks like end but it is a process of beginning.

**Knowing Death**

Death panics us, I know as much as you know. It panics me too. But why? Why is death so fearful to us? Hollywood actress, **Angelina Jolie**, has to say, **"If I think more about death than some other people, it is probably because I love life more than they do"**. We all fear death for the same reason as Angelina. Because we love life and we love it too much! And we fear death because we think it will snatch away 'life' from our grip, it will filch life off our tight embrace. Death appears to us as an unknown villainess in the drama of *zindagi* that will usurp the best things we possess.

But none of us has ever met that 'villainess' and when we will meet her, it will be too late to come back and describe her face to our fellows. But even before we have an encounter with death, perhaps we can strive to know if she is cruel or kind, hateful or affectionate, harsh or honeyed; and whether she is really a villainess! In this process to know 'Death', we all can draw upon the perceptions of our own life and teachings of the great Messengers who uttered nothing without the permission of the Almighty.

We don't know if death comes to take away life from us or to bestow a new life. We don't even know if life is the beginning of death or death is the beginning of life, in the same way as we don't know which petal of the beautiful rose is the first petal and which is the last. We really don't know if, in the beginning, we all lived dead and 'hidden' in our Creator and then appeared on the stage of life by His divine will or we died in Him as life eternals, never to die again. **Tagore** said: **"Death is not extinguishing the light; it is putting out the lamp because dawn has come"**. Maybe, what we consider the night of life is really the dawn of a new existence!

Death does not come to take away life from us, even though it appears like that. It just opens new doors to a greater life, a larger world. In the 'Seven Valleys' there is a story of a lover whose condition had become extremely deplorable in long separation from his beloved. Like a *divānā*, a madcap, a *Majnoon* of love, he wandered from street to street looking for only one thing: a glimpse of his beloved. One night when he could no longer bear the grief and was intensely restless, he made his way to a market street in his clumsy dress and shaggy hair. The royal watchman thought him to be a nuisance wandering out in the odd hours and ran after him. The lover's condition was already frail and pale. He hadn't taken a morsel of food since many days and was too weak and desolate. Yet, when the watchman shouted and ran after him, he also ran, cursing him and praying to God to save him from this 'envoy of death'. As he was fleeing with all his might, with the watchman behind him like the hound of death, the way ended and there was a wall in front of him. Finding no other way to escape, he scaled the wall with all his might and found himself on the other side which was a lavish garden, full of wonderful flowers. And there he saw his beloved holding a lamp in her hand and looking for her lost ring. With utmost joy, he closed his eyes and thanked God for sending that 'Messenger of life' after him who brought this cherished union with his beloved.

We are afraid of the 'chasing of death' and curse her every moment because, in our ignorant opinion, she is inflicting torture upon us, depriving us of the beauties and bounties of life, taking away from us all the attractions that we set our heart upon. Maybe, the reality is different! Maybe, death is like that watchman driving us to that endpoint, to that ultimate wall of life, beyond which we will find our Beloved, where greater attractions are waiting for us, where love is to be found in a fuller measure, where we are to receive the delight of our soul in the Garden of Everlasting Eden!

> *The delight that comes from women, offspring, hoards of gold and silver, horses and cattle, and realties is though attractive for the humankind, they are comfortable only for the worldly life. With Allah there is a more splendid abode.*
>
> (The Quran, III:14)

Thus, a far better and more enriched life lies beyond this mortal world which we enter through the gateway of death. How can we curse Death if she is so kind upon us! Won't we rather believe in this assurance of Baha'u'llah:

*O Son of the Supreme! I have made death a messenger of joy to thee. Wherefore dost thou grieve? I made the light to shed on thee its splendour. Why dost thou veil thyself therefrom?*

(The Hidden Words, 32)

Why we cannot see death as a 'messenger of joy'? Why do we lament when a close person dies? That's because we feel an unbridgeable gap of separation between ourselves and that departed soul. But our dear ones who left the world are not 'lost', for the simple reason that 'spirit' cannot be lost, energy cannot be destroyed. This is also not the truth that we won't see them again. If we have true love for them and they had for us, it is not possible that the intensity of that love will be of no avail.

**Ehaloka and Parloka**

We have to believe that there are two worlds in existence. One is the world of matter and the other is the world of spirit. The world of matter is destructible but the world of spirit is inexhaustible. Eyes are lost but the sight cannot be burnt in fire. Nostrils are stuffed with the soil of the grave, but the smell our soul smelt is there with the soul lingering on. Skin will lose its charm one day, but the feelings will last. My ears will no longer be in this world but the melody of the voice of my beloved will remain ringing in my core? Who can take that from me? Death does not prevent us from acquiring the presence of those whom we loved on this earth. There is no separation at all. They shall surely:

*....associate and commune intimately one with another, and shall be so closely associated in their lives, their aspirations, their aims and strivings as to be even as one soul. (They are) well aware of one another's state and condition, and are united in the bonds of intimacy and fellowship. Such a state, however, must depend upon their faith and their conduct. They that are of the same grade and station are fully aware of one another's capacity, character, accomplishments and merits. They that are of a lower grade, however, are incapable of comprehending adequately the station, or of estimating the merits, of those that rank above them. ..... The souls of the infidels, however, shall - and to this I bear witness - when breathing their last be made aware of the good things that have escaped them, and shall bemoan their plight, and shall humble themselves before God.*

(Gleanings from the Writings of Baha'u'llah, www.bahai.org)

Death releases a boundless life for us. As we can see in dreams, we feel much more freedom than when we are awake. In conscious state we can't travel far-off places without material means, but in that trance of dream we can move freely in a vast world. Even though our eyes, nostrils, ears, mouth, hands and feet are all inactive, we can see spectacular views, smell fragrances as real, hear the warbling of rivers and chirping of birds, taste sumptuous foods, touch things with true feelings and walk smoothly even on mountains. When an ordinary state of sleeping can unleash such extra-physical capacities, how much powerful must the soothing lap of death be, with its indescribable peace and disembodied potencies! This world is very beautiful but death allows us to walk into a world that is even more beautiful.

Death is not a horrible fact. This is also testified by our mind's usual perception of death. Everyone knows that death is inevitable, even a child knows, yet how much focus does our mind give on it? Until and unless we forcefully dictate our mind to focus on 'death', it does not even accept the existence of death. Mind is basically a machine to help our survival. As such, it should always focus on death because death threatens our survival. But we understand by our own daily experience that mind does not show a 'caring' attention to death. Even now when 'death' has been mentioned so many times, how much afraid are you? This is really a wondrous thing. In the '**Mahābhārata**', there is a chapter in which Yudhisthira, who was a great scholar among the Pandavas, answers some highly metaphysical questions asked by a demigod. One of the questions of the demigod is: **"What is surprise?"** The essence of Yudhisthira's reply is that **even though everyone watches daily that death is devouring scores of people one by one, those who are spared till now don't think their turn will come, too.** What can be a better proof of the non-importance of death in this vivacious life pattern?

Many people who met near-death experience (NDE) have been interviewed and their observations scientifically recorded. In most experiences, they describe a feeling of freedom from time and space which, in itself, fills the person with a sense of liberation. Many narrated that they felt themselves to be immortal beings and were very happy as they could go anywhere freely. Others have said that in their near-death experience they entered a world and felt they had already been there and the life of the earth was very brief and insignificant in that comparison. There is no ageing, no wearing and tearing, everything is fresh and juvenile, bright and new. Many NDE-subjects reported that they met their close relatives and loved ones. All these experiences are a verbatim match with the details in great Scriptures regarding a World which is a "**home of peace**" that "**will remain forever**", with its "**Gardens of delight**", where "**toil will not touch**", and "**where every wish is immediately fulfilled**" (Islam); where there is "**neither hunger nor thirst**", "**neither heat nor cold**", "**no old age**", "**delightful fragrance and sounds**", "**close association of the Lord**" (Hinduism); where we have "**life everlasting**", in that "**holy place**", "**the heavenly Jerusalem**" (Christianity); characterised by "**great joy**", "**the place where souls will recognise other souls**", in "**closeness to God**" (Baha'i Faith); the "**Pure Land**" (Buddhism) and the "**New Earth**" (Judaism). Is this not more exciting than this earthly life?

**True Meaning of Life and Death**

When we understand this true nature of death and realise that 'spirit' (soul) cannot be destructed even when the 'matter' (body) is dissipated, and when we strongly feel in our heart that we all basically belong to a spiritual world where, as **Chuang Tzu** said, **"Birth is not a beginning and death is not an end"**, we come a step forward from the previous level of understanding where we saw two worlds: one of destructible matter and the other of everlasting spirit. Now, we start realising this monistic truth that only God exists and everything else is merely an appearance. Then this world of matter looks like the shadow of the sky in the lake. We see moons and stars in the lake but they never exist there, they exist in the sky. Whatever we see in this material world, is but a reflection of the spiritual kingdom. They are for a meaning, they are for a purpose, they are there to teach us the truths of the spiritual world. So is death and so is life.

We come to realise one day that life is very beautiful, very picturesque, fascinating, young and marvellous, velvety and cosy, pleasant and rosy, so superb, so soulful that our heart, overwhelmed and enraptured, sings along with **William Brighty Rands**:

**Great, wide, beautiful, wonderful World,**
**With the wonderful water round you curled,**
**And the wonderful grass upon your breast,**
**World, you are beautifully drest.**

Yet behind this veil of beauty, something deep inside our being is still athirst, craving for Greater Beauty. One day we realise that this endless caravan of charm and fascination is still there but our own time is up and we must go. One day this truth, uttered by **Bhartrihari**, becomes clear:

**Time is not passing, we are passing**
**Desires are not ageing, we are ageing.**

One day every atom of our being testifies to this truth that behind the gardens of these beauties of the world, there are also sobbing graveyards; beside these flowers there are thorns; behind these pledges of *wafa*, there are deviations to indecent proposals, amidst these merrymaking fiestas there are a thousand tears of starving children, and betwixt these parades of glamour there are a hundred conspiracies of ungodly ambitions. It is in such moments of realisation that we feel we spent our whole life counting the shining stars on the rippling waves of the lake, whereas the true stars shone just overhead in the sky of the Eternal Reality. Then we take death truly as a fairy of joy, and holding her hands we soar to those heights of life where beauties never fade nor does our youthfulness and innocence. That day we realise that this earthly life was not meant for us to stay here in these 'lovely, dark and deep woods' but we had to keep our promise and go miles away from here to meet the Beloved.

### Attachment and Detachment

Those who do not believe in previous birth or reincarnation, have a very solid blame on those who believe in it. They say that the theory of reincarnation is basically based on 'material attachment' of those who believe in it. Since they want to come back to enjoy this life again and again, therefore they want to believe in such (bodily) life after death. Very true they are! Those who toss such ungrateful thoughts perhaps never loved

God. Or they loved on a 'narrow margin' where God was accepted but His world was not. They say that they love the Artist, but loving His art is 'attachment'!

Attachment and appreciation are two different things. No doubt, this life is not always pleasant. Sure, afflictions outlast delights, pains outnumber pleasures. Undoubtedly, this material world is not true but an appearance, but how lovely this appearance is! The pearls spark for a while but, oh! what a dazzling sparkle they shed! We have short moments of love but ask those who lived those moments. Will they barter even a thousands heavens with a kiss of their beloved? Life is good, life is great not because life is good and life is great, but because He Who created it is good and great. Those who respect that Creator, that matchless Artist, will not utter, even in the utmost privacy of their own serene conscience that O God, don't let me come to this 'ugly' and 'bitter' world again! Life may be a tart cup of poison, but those who are Christ at heart, will pray humbly in these words only:

> *"Father, if it is Your will, take this cup away from Me; nevertheless, not My will but Yours be done."*
>
> (The Bible, Luke, 22:42)

Loving this world, accepting it in its wholeness of pleasure and pain, being grateful to its blissful and morose moments that led us to realise the truths of the spiritual world, acknowledging thankfully those countless opportunities that we could find only in this world for the upliftment of our soul, through the vicissitudes of bright and dark days and nights of this worldly life, is not to be termed as 'attachment' but 'appreciation'.

If this world had not been there, how could we know God? How could we know the insipidity of matter, without knowing the matter? Denouncing the world without reaching the sublime heights of spirituality is like denying the ladder before climbing atop. It is like telling a beggar about the worthlessness of wealth. The one who has never tasted a crumb of delicious food, will never accept that food is nothing but a false matter, a hallucination. That 'hallucination' is his life! But when he has become rich and the most delicious foods of the world are lavishly available to him, he understands how all his illnesses are due to these foods.

In an earlier chapter, the following verse from the Geetā is given:

> *The one who fell from the path of 'yoga', goes to heavenly realms and after a prolonged stay in those realms, he is born in the house of a noble and virtuous person.*
>
> (6: 41)

Here Lord Krishna is referring to a practising 'yogi' who observed every possible self-discipline, self-control, and austerity to achieve spiritual perfection, but ultimately deviated from his goal. Arjuna asked Him about the destiny of such a seeker (or a 'yogi') on the path of perfection.

What Krishna wants to say is that our previous efforts on the path of virtue are not lost. As such that seeker who deviated in the last time will still start his journey in his next birth from the point he had left previously. But why does he go to heavenly realms and stay there for many years and enjoy in the 'heavens' the same sensual pleasures which were the cause of his 'falling', before being born in the house of a noble person? Why he cannot immediately born in the house of a noble person or family of a yogi and start his further journey thence?

The answer is simple. The 'yogi' who deviated from the path of 'yoga' was still wandering in the sensual world. That is why he 'fell'. If he is to be born again immediately in a virtuous family, still his sense-thirsty soul will not let him grab the girdle of detachment. He will deviate again and again. It is, therefore, necessary that he should be placed in the 'heavens of sensual delights' till he knows how fake and tasteless these delights are. Only then can he proceed further.

The road to God goes through this world and that is why He has made souls immortal: to be born again, again and again, again and again, till the foods of desire are fully consumed in the fire of this Sufi knowledge that "Only God exists; He is in all things, and all things are in Him." And then, desires become useless because all desires are already met in the most desired. And then, this world remains no more meaningful for the soul, because all worlds dissolve in God. In the worlds he sees God and in God he sees all the worlds.

*The one who knows God in His essence, is no longer concerned with other knowledge (The*

*Veda), in the same way as the one who found an ocean has nothing to do with a pond.*

(The Geeta, 2:46)

Then be it life or death, it has no meaning for him. **Attachment** and **detachment** both die in him. Love and hatred are unknown words to him as he is lost in his inner bliss. That day Death comes near that soul, and bringing her moist lips close, she gives him a deep kiss, deeper than a beloved could ever stud on the lips of her lover and whispers: "Today I die to live in you forever". And eternal life begins thence!

## 12

# Detachment and Surrender

> *Resign the care of your destiny to higher powers, be genuinely indifferent as to what becomes of it all and you will find not only that you gain a perfect inward relief, but often also, in addition, the particular goods you sincerely thought you were renouncing.*
>
> — *William James*

Birds fly with two wings. If we compare the journey of our life to the flight of a mystic bird, the two wings that this bird possesses are: **Destiny** and **Free Will**. The one wing is 'unseen', the other is our control. The flight takes the flapping of these two wings together.

There is a Punjabi proverb: **'Apni tod nibhaiye, ohdi oh jāne'** (Do your best, He knows His course). We are all just actors on the stage. Our parts are already envisioned, dialogues written, songs composed, climaxes already in place! But we don't know what is written. We are not given the ken to look into the future and know beforehand what our role is going to be! Had we known it, this journey would have been very uncomfortable, very threatening, unexciting and fearful. We could know beforehand who are going to love us, as well as, who are going to cheat, who are going to put a crown on our head and who are going to heap ignominies, whose death and separation is going to toll our soul and which advents and unions are to thrill our hearts. For the reasons best known to Him, God has kept the future mysterious to us and we have only one option: to assume that it is we who think, decide and act.

**Ideas Retained: Life Continues**

The truth is that what we 'think' today is also guided by what we 'thought' in our previous life. A person who was, for example, a butcher in his last birth, cannot suddenly become a Martin Luther King in this birth and start to 'think' about non-violence. Thus, even our 'thought' is a part of destiny. People think in different ways in this world and as they think, so they act, and so they attract their further destiny. There is a fine thread weaving together our 'previous' existence with our existence now in a natural way, and we think that 'we' are 'thinking', and we think that 'we' are doing!

When we died in our previous life, we left our corporeal body which was burnt or buried. But what happened of those songs we sang so vehemently, those desires we fostered so strongly, those thirsts which made us impatient from the depth of our heart? I had touched the Jasmines with silky petals and my fingers said 'oh, this same smoothness I must always feel!' On the crimson horizons of my dreams and hopes, I saw the true colours of my life dancing with the beams of the dawn. I loved life so dearly and so passionately that I welcomed that girl of immortal beauty and after finding her I need not find God as His beauty was wrapped in her! In that soul of my friend I found a 'jagged part' of my own soul. How lovely that life was with those crystalline fountains falling from the snow-covered mount, with those green pastures with innocently grazing rams, that mystic song echoing in the dusk time from a far-off place from the lips of that young widow who lost her man in a war! And you say, my life is finished? Death has taken away all my sounds and senses? My songs are stolen, my Jasmines are lost?

Damn go! Damn go! Damn go from here! My desires will never die. You burnt my body, you threw my members before tigers and wolves, you submerged me in the river, buried me in the grave. Huh! Lo! I am born again; in a new body, now don't ask what this body looks like! Don't play with words that this is a 'heavenly body' or a 'corporeal body'. Which body do you have in your dream: Heavenly or Corporeal? Which body takes you, O the Sleeping Corpse on the Couch, to Mexico and London, without an aeroplane, with no formalities of passport and visa? Which lips tasted the sweetness of your love in that dream? Which eyes saw his or her beauty in that transported world? Which 'senses' satisfied you more than you are satisfied in reality? I have the same body wherever I am born. Call it spiritual or call it real but one thing is true that I can satisfy my desires with this body. Just one thing is clear, until and unless I have touched my Jasmine to my utmost satisfaction, and embraced my beloved till my breath stops, I will be born again and again.

When the soul travels from this world, it travels with all its powerful longings, passions, desires, bereavements, visualisations, smells, feelings, emotions and all similar properties. These are the very things that cause us to be born again so that we can meet those desires on the planes of reality.

> *As the wind carries the fragrance from its source, in the same way the senses and the mind are also abstracted into the soul when the being departs from his body, and are transported to the new physical form.*
>
> (The Geetā, 15: 8)

*Shariram yad wāpnoti yachchāpyutkrāmat ishwarah;*
*Grihitvaitāni sanyāti vāyuh gandh anivāshayāt.*

Desires have only one antidote – Detachment. According to the Geeta, when an action is performed free from attachment with the outcome, it becomes an action that liberates us from the bonds of desires. When desires are thus exhausted in the fire of detachment, the soul regains its original state of divine contentment. It becomes like a candle burning in its tranquil singleness, unaffected by the winds of passions and desires, lusts and ambitions, angers and envies.

> *If the mind becomes balanced and detached, and comes to dwell in its own true home, imbued with the Fear of God, then it enjoys the essence*

*of supreme spiritual wisdom; it shall never feel hunger again.*

(Guru Granth Sāhib)

Then there is no need of birth, there is no need of 'body' for fulfilment of desires, and no place for '*karma*'. It is that state when the soul has obtained the heights of the realms of God that is far above heavens. It is the world which, as **Krishna** depicts, **is not lighted by the Sun, the Moon or the Fire and from where no soul ever returns to this world below.**

However, it seems too difficult to gain that state of detachment. We, ordinary beings as we are, cannot imagine lifting up our mind to such a plinth of calmness where it inspires us to 'act' but seek 'no result', because almost all actions start from thought (desire). If we have no desire, there would be no action.

It is this very crux of the world of action where our belief in destiny comes to our aid. Believing in destiny does not mean that we have no free will. Believing in destiny means there is a 'divine will' greater than our individual free will, and that divine will is never, not for a single moment, working against us. Believing in destiny means that a far-sighted Providence is at work in my individual life, a Providence that is, in the words of Baha'u'llah, **'more friendly to me than I am to myself'**. Believing in destiny is a matter of faith which sets us free from limited individual anxieties, liberates us from too much pining on our burdens, and fills us with a sense of detachment.

When we believe in destiny and, at the same time, trust in our God-given 'free will', we get ready to flap this wing of free will to say that 'I want to fly'. Soon after, the other 'invisible' wing of destiny also flutters. The cycle goes on and the flight becomes possible. Perhaps, in this flight, the unseen wings of destiny will take us to a destination that we had not thought of, but one thing is sure, the place where we will reach will be 'dearer to our heart'.

Believing in destiny and leaving our affairs in the hands of the Unseen is not 'indifference', nor lack of zeal for action. Detachment does not mean depriving our action from being goal-oriented or robbing it of its warmth and fervour. It simply means 'not being a slave of our desire'. It symbolises our inner calmness even if things go contrary, so that we can restart with a fresh zeal, like an innocent child whose sand-house was demolished by the waves, and he cried a little, wept a little, and then wiping his tears with his tiny fingers, sat near the shore to build a new sand-house:

*As by the entry of rivers the ocean is not turbulent, so the soul that remains undisturbed by the various incoming desires attains peace, not the one which runs after desires.*

(The Geetā, 2:70)

*Āpuryamānam achala pratishtham*
*Samudra māpah pravishanti yadvat;*
*Tadvatkāmā yam pravishanti sarve*
*Sa shāntim wāpnoti na kāmakāmi.*

Detachment means doing everything with utmost perfection, with deepest feelings, with the best possible efforts and then 'releasing' the action off the pitch of desire. Detachment is like shooting an arrow to hit its target. We focus on the aim, put the arrow on the bow, set it to the target, and pull the string with our fullest might. But beware! There is a point and if you keep pulling more, you will break the string and the arrow will fall down losing its tense potency. There is a time to 'pull' the string of desire, then there is a time to 'release' the arrow of action. If we keep too much attention on the 'result', we will rather repel the result.

Detachment has one more grave significance and meaning. It is allowing God and universe to respond to our desires in 'perfect and divine timing'. It is believing that every desire, if expressed strongly and with faith, is bound to be honoured in this universe. Our part is to wait patiently 'in the time of the universe' and not 'in our time'. Our time is very small, comprised of some minutes, some days, some countable years, but God lives in infinite time, the universe is floating in eternity. A prayer that you made today may be answered by God in His 'one day' that can be a span of several births for you. If you are a divine child, refuse to live in minutes, weeks, fortnights, months and years. Live in eternity, pray in eternity, expect in eternity!

Every desire is fulfilled here. There is no "NO" in this generous universe. It is willing to bestow upon you all that you ask. But there is one thing that the universe wants from you, 'Faith', unchangeable faith, faith that has determination, faith that is not bound to change even when everything appears to change, faith that cannot waiver from the ups and downs of time, topsy and turvy of kismet. Since the universe is nothing but an expression of divine energy, weak resolves are not entertained in this divine world. The fake currencies of 'doubts' cannot buy anything in this Kingdom of God. If you want wealth, ask it and it will be given, and have faith that it will be given. Be definite. Ask a definite thing. Then believe and wait 'truly' and not with such cheating motives that 'ok let me see it works or not'. This is not 'faith', this is 'trying'. If John wants Christina, let him ask from the universe Christina and only Christina. The universe will try to 'negotiate', in its own invisible ways working through John's mind and incidents of his life, whether he can settle with Nina or Zena. If John's love for Christina is so fickle that any Nina or Zena would be okay for him, the universe does not care such incredible Johns. If Nina wants Ramesh, let her ask for Ramesh and only Ramesh. Let her not settle with John or Saleem. This is the way the universe works through the power of Faith. "**Faith bears fruit**" and "**those who doubt are destroyed**" (The Geetā). "**Be not of those who doubt**" (Baha'u'llah: The Tablet of Ahmad). "**Let him ask in faith, with no doubting ... for let not that man suppose that he will receive anything from the Lord**" (The Epistle of James). "**I answer the prayer of the suppliant ... Let him hear My call and trust in Me**". (The Quran, II:186).

In Buddhism, '*Saddha*' (Faith) is the first of the 'five spiritual faculties' and one of the 'seven treasures'.

Naturally, when Faith is such a powerful property that it can attract any wealth to us, fulfil any of our desires, it must be a precious 'treasure' kept at a secure place. That secure place is God. We can draw as much faith as we want from God. We ourselves cannot be a storehouse of such a mighty wealth. In other words, our faith wavers only for one reason: we look at our own weaknesses and incapacities. We depend on the mercies of people. It is true that we are very weak and incapable creatures. It is true that no man can be so kind on us that we can depend on him. It is true that we feel tired and like giving up at times. However, if we look upon God, we draw immense Faith and we know that nothing is impossible if He wants.

> *But they that wait upon the Lord shall renew their strength; they shall mount up with wings as eagles; they shall run, and not be weary, and they shall walk, and not faint.*
>
> (Isaiah 40:31)

When we 'detach' ourselves from our poor capacities and 'attach' with the immense power of God, wonders happen. Then we are not poor Johns and Christinas, Rameshes and Ninas, Saleems and Zenas; we become a part of the mighty Ocean of endless possibilities, sustained and supported by the Indomitable Power that infuses new life into all things:

> *I am the royal Falcon on the arm of the Almighty. I unfold the drooping wings of every broken bird and start it on its flight.*
>
> (Baha'u'llah : LAWH-I-MAQSÚD )

The life of each Messenger of God reflects the vitality of Faith. In the Bible we read several stories about the power of faith that Jesus Christ wielded, including the story in which He was walking on the sea. All His disciples saw Him and were afraid that it was a ghost. But Peter asked Him if he also could come to Him walking on water and He said 'Yes'. Peter was full of faith and that is why he dared to ask if he could come to Him walking on water. Others did not even ask as they did not believe. Yet when Peter put his feet on the sea and realised the boisterous storm, he started sinking. Jesus held him and scolded: **"O you of little faith, why do you doubt?"** There are very few 'Peters' among us, even their faith dwindles in storms of life. But if we have complete faith in God, we will pass all turbulent seas.

**Rāma** was ousted by His own stepmother but with the help of an untrained army of monkeys He defeated a king whose power was indomitable in his time. **Krishna** was nurtured among simple cowherds and yet He became the most dynamic power of His era. **Abraham** was outwardly helpless but when God was with Him, He vanquished the mighty armies of Nimrod. **Moses** had no weapons except his simple staff but with the strength of God arrayed in His side, He thwarted the powerful Pharaoh. **Jesus Christ** was a humble and ordinary person for people but He was victorious through His faith in God. **Muhammad** was born among the most savage people of the world but with God's might, He established a kingdom and civilised a barbarous nation. **Baha'u'llah** was kept in exile throughout His life, but He established a stirring world religion flourishing today in almost all countries of the globe. If faith is there, what is impossible? Ask in faith, ask in definiteness, ask with determination, and forget it! Get detached! This is your entire role. The rest is God's.

Well, what is 'Detachment' from one aspect is surrender from the other; they are two words with the same meaning in different perspectives. Detachment limits itself to forsaking the 'results' of the actions, yet a raiment of desire is still there. If there are no 'desires', from what are you 'detached'? Being 'detached' itself means that a 'desire' exists. Detachment is very praiseworthy but it is a negative concept yet; having no attachment. But there is a stage of development for each soul, a stage loftier than Detachment. That is the stage of Surrender.

When the soul reaches that stage of Surrender, he neither renounces nor accepts. He becomes a tool in the hands of the Almighty, free from his individual desires as such and only responding to his pure inspirations, spending his life in loving His creation and serving each and all. He has no self of his own and no desires for his own sake. He knows everything in their entity. He admits in his heart that there is no 'support' in this changing world that can support him, no friend whose love will abide, no delight that can last forever, no union that has no separation, no promise that can't be broken, no heart that cannot change, no solace that can quench his burning thirst! Knowing the futility of this fleeting world, he holds the 'Firmest Handhold' of God Who will never leave him. That is the end of the journey of the soul from all the realms of desires. There, in that heaven of self-contentment, he finds even greater rewards with God, and: "**there shall no fear come upon them, neither shall they grieve**" (The Quran, I:112). This is the world of emancipation from where there is no return and there is complete absolution from all the sins and bonds of 'karma': **Abandon all other concerns and seek refuge in Me alone. Don't worry at all as I will set you free from all your sins.** – Lord Krishna in The Geeta, 18:66.

*Sarva dharmān parityajya māmekam sharanam braj;*
*Aham tvā sarva pāpebhyo mokshyishyāmi mā shuchah.*

The essence of knowledge is to understand that this mortal life, this material world, is not the ultimate goal of the soul. But it is in these mortal worlds of God where the soul finds its expressions and receives the vehicle of body to act for its own emancipation. Wandering through the enchanting woods of desires and ambitions, a time comes in the journey of the soul when it witnesses the futility of desires and craves for its union with its Greater Self. It is through this aspiration of the soul that the cycle of life and death ceases.

**

13

# Did I Exist Before

*Man is a spiritual being -- a soul, in other words -- and this soul takes on different bodies from life to life on earth in order to ultimately arrive at such perfect knowledge, through repeated experience, as to enable one to assume a body fit to be the dwelling-place of a Mahatma or perfected soul.*

*— Helena Petrovna Blavatsky*

In late 60's, when I was living with my mother in Morwa, a small settlement in Samastipur district of Bihar, India, I was pretty young, but there is a memory of that early childhood which still lingers in my mind. Around those years, a Hindi film (with actors – Shashi Kapoor, Nanda) was released – **Jab Jab Phool Khile**, directed by Suraj Prakash. There was a song in this film – "**Ek thā Gul or ek thee Bulbul, dono chaman mein rahte the; hai ye kahāni bilkul sachchi, mere nānā kahte the**". It literally means: '**There was a Gul (Flower)**

**and a Bulbul (Nightingale), both lived in a garden; and this story is true, as my maternal grandfather used to say**'. The touching song, sung in soulful voice depicted a petty love story in which the *Gul* (Flower) was a shy lover who could never express his love to the lovely *Bulbul* (Nightingale) but his love was very deep and true. They happily lived in the garden feeling their 'silent' love day after day. Once a *Sayyād* (Bird-catcher) ensnared the Bulbul and took her away. For the love-intoxicated *Gul*, it was a soul-stirring event. He faded, and wailed for his beloved *Bulbul*. So pensive were his laments and so strong was his desire to reunite with his *Bulbul* that the whole universe was stirred up and the *Bulbul* was released to fly back to him. In the end, there's a message in the song: 'No matter you live or die, your love must always be like the *Gul* and the *Bulbul*'.

Now for a child of 4-5 years, especially in those days when movies, television and other modern-age devices used to help in maturing the children prematurely were completely missing in that rural area of a backward district of India, it was not possible to understand the meaning or feel the emotions as conveyed in the song. I had not even watched the film but there was something in my heart that related itself so badly with the song that I used to burst into tears. I used to weep so sorely that my tears could not be controlled. I remember that I used to hide myself behind a cabinet, door, curtains, box, etc. or go in the backyard so that no one can see me crying like that. Yet, my mother knew it and whenever this song was played on radio, she would come looking for me just to find me behind a curtain, all wet in tears.

Years went by and I saw that film later when I was in my college. It was a story of love between a poor '*shikārā*' (houseboat) owner of Kashmir and a rich tourist girl. Even that time when I was watching the film, I didn't have a faint idea that a 'tourist' will come and infatuate my soul so deeply for ever!

**Raed Life: Hidden Meaning**

Then I remember one more impression. It was around 1970 when I was in Darbhangā. There was a Muslim beggar boy of 6-7 years who used to come to our house and my mother would give him money or something to eat. Whenever I saw that boy, I was filled with a strange feeling of love and compassion, as if he was my own part, my brother. Many times, when he used to come, my mother was not there. Though I could give him nothing, I would feel a strong urge to hug him and cry a lot. In such moments, he too would just stand still feeling the warmth of my tears flowing down my cheeks, and he was himself crying. What was this strange connection and why? There were many other poor boys of his age in Darbhangā.

In the year 2000, it was first time ever in my life that I had to go inside the Iranian Embassy at Barakhambā Road, New Delhi, for a work. As soon as I went inside, I felt I've come inside a world already known to me. The building, the inner structures, even the ambience and smell, all seemed to be very familiar to me. But I was sure I had never visited that place before, at least in this life.

There is also a different world in which the 'realities' of the past life look into our eyes, the world of dreams. Since time immemorial, dreams have been closely related with the unexplored areas of human soul where pains and sufferings, raptures and delights, passions and desires of a past life surface out, in hidden guises, for our cursory observation. We see in our dreams diverse worlds that we never saw before, people we never met, situation that we never even thought of in our current life. Some of these dreams deeply relate with a past-life trauma that keeps haunting down the ages in our birth cycles. They make an indelible mark in our subconscious entity, so much so that they are able to paralyse our current living, dreams, desires and achievements.

I know one of my friends who used to see a sequence of dreams throughout his life though he could not understand how these dreams related with his present life. In one of such dreams, he used to find himself in tall buildings of ancient architecture, such as relics on a fort, a ruined palace or haveli, a rampart, or an old-fashioned multi-storey building. In his dreams, he would somehow find himself on the top of these buildings, having no idea how he got there. All gates and exits were closed, no stairs to get down. He was confused and afraid as he looked down from that frightening height. And then there was a pause in the dream and he would find that 'somehow' he had got down. How? He never knew.

Another dream was about his travelling with family in a train and passing through a number of railway stations he had never known in life, mostly snow-covered areas in which names of stations were seldom clear due to mist or fog. And the train would stop at a lonely station. Leaving his family in the compartment, he would come down to find some coffee or tea. He will wander a little on the platform forgetful of time, and on his return the train had left. He stood there on that lonely station with a feeling of profound bereavement, unbridgeable separation, a state of bewilderment to which he, and he alone, was the witness.

In yet another dream sequence, he used to see himself falling into an abysmal depth, into a well with no end, like a dark tunnel!

In his present life, he could not trace any trauma, any feeling of loss or bereavement, any love for archaeological places or buildings, or any hidden fear of downfall that could be logically related to these dreams. Yet these dreams continued, in a systematic order, with slight changes in people and places but always with the same intensity of feelings and every time leaving a deep impact on his mind.

Many dreams like these often refer to some phobias, nightmares, panic attacks, abandonment, accidents, depressions, tragically broken relationships, guilt and chronic problems of body or mind, sufferings and struggles and many unfading memories of such events following from one's previous lives. These phobias and reminiscences of the past lives are sometimes easily recalled in childhood days, not only because childhood is close to previous life but also because children have not yet developed that wise 'logical' power of mind and are receptive to messages from the unseen worlds. Many children, not only in India where belief in previous life existence is popular but also in Christian and Muslim countries where such beliefs are 'forcefully shut', have clearly reported about incidences of the past lives. These events are so many and so authentically proven that it would require several volumes of books to be written just on that topic and regretfully I have to refrain from dwelling on the subject. However, if you want to wonder on this mysterious world of dreams, keep a "Dream Diary" close to your bed and always note down the bizarre dreams you see. You will forget them too soon, so note down quickly, as soon as you get up after the dream. You will wonder how so many of your dreams relate to events that will happen in your life years later, and many dreams will just leave you with a feeling of deprivation that has no root in your present life, but they allude to some lingering moments of a remote past, far beyond this life.

**Dreams are Windows**

Many psychologists believe that dreams 'talk' to us in a 'symbolic' language and want to tell us about the things we have missed in our life, past or present or the attractions and tragedies that await us in the forthcoming lives.

Dreams are not just expressions of our suppressed desires, as Sigmund Freud said. In Hinduism, the seers had a clear knowledge about dreams, and in some of the Vedas and Upanishadas we can find scientific explanations about dreams. For example, in **Brihadāranyak Upanishad** (4/3/9), dreams are said to be such states of consciousness where two worlds meet: the material and the spiritual. Our dreams are 'windows' through which we can see beyond this life.

What is said in **Brihadāranyak**, is further confirmed by science. Our mind functions basically in three vibrational states: conscious, subconscious, and unconscious. These states have a respective energy wave patterns. For example, the conscious mind (the state when you are reading this book) functions at a vibration range of above 14 Hz of **Beta** waves. This is the logical state of mind. The subconscious mind vibrates at a range between 4-7 Hz of **Theta** waves. This is the state when logical faculty of mind is completely subdued and there is a connection with the 'unseen' world, a state of mind when such treasures of wisdom are revealed as cannot be grasped by a conscious mind. This is our 'Dream State'. The unconscious mind is completely in sleeping state vibrating at 0.5-4 Hz of **Delta** waves. Even in this state of mind, the subconscious mind remains active and takes care of our respiration, blood circulation and other necessary functions of our system. Between the Beta and Theta states of mind, there is the **Alpha** state of vibration between 7-14 Hz. Most of our 'sublime' thoughts, ideas and inspirations come in this state.

Through all these various vistas of life opening up to us in our dreams and realities, a vital truth is mutely revealed to us: **the life we are living now did not begin**

**just on this plane nor by death it is going to culminate here, on this planet.** We are visitors from a spiritual world, sent here on a mission after fulfilling which we will return to our eternal abode.

Each one of us, if truly sincere to himself or herself, will trace many such dreams and events in our lives that allude to our 'connection' to a world hitherto unknown. Each one of us has seen such miraculous dreams in his or her life in which he or she has 'travelled' to the 'other world' where a part of him or her exists 'now', existed in the Past or will exist in the Future. Each one of us will recall from his or her own impressions of life how a particular place, a particular person, scenery, a song, an event, a building, a child, an object, a memory or anything suddenly 'invited' him or her to refresh an 'old' memory that goes beyond the time and space of this world. Truth dares to look into the eyes of each one of us, but most of us just jerk our head and go away saying, 'ah! I felt I was drowsy.' Yet, there is no answer in the logical world of these wise non-drowsy people as to why each one in this world is attracted to different things, different people? Why all of us don't share the same attraction?

And there is no answer also to this fact that why different people are born with different aptitudes? Why it is so that someone is born with literary talents even though he or she did not receive a planned education in the area of literature? Why someone becomes a veteran sportsman even though his or her personal circumstances are so constrained? Many international players were born in such poor families where they didn't have enough to feed themselves, much less to buy bats and rackets. Why someone, though forced into a different life and profession, knows for sure that he is born to be an actor and pursues his goal? Why two people in the same circumstances drift to two different directions in life? Why it so happens that though apples keep falling straight on the earth from centuries, suddenly a Newton picks up the mystery of gravity? Why is it so although everyday people are born here, they grow old, fall ill and die and yet only one out of them becomes a Gautam Buddha?

For many, there is a preset answer for all such questions: it is all our situations and how we react to them. But, my brother! Why are there 'different situations' and why are there 'different reactions'? I agree that 'thoughts become things' and 'we become what we think'. But why even two twin brothers born in the same family, to the same parents, receiving same food and water, nutrition and education, atmosphere and surrounding, have two different thoughts? Why they have two different destinies? What are the elements that decide 'A' will think like this and 'B' will think like that?

Why everyone thrown out of the train does not choose to be Mahatma Gandhi? Why so many failures of life make one Abraham Lincoln and the other becomes a robber of the Chambal Valley? Why are people born with different mindsets? Why we fall in love with certain people? Why some people and things repel us even though they have apparently done no harm to us? Why we have unknown phobias having no root in this life?

I strongly and unshakably believe that each soul here is commissioned with a task: to know God and find Him. There is no other purpose of creation, and each soul has to accomplish this task on its own, inescapably! Until and unless this 'spiritual mission' is fulfilled, there is no peace, there is no full stop, there is no escape, no salvation.

However, this task is so tremendous. One lifespan cannot be sufficient for fulfilling it. When God created human soul, He cast His own image in him. When he appeared in these mortal worlds, he was a resplendent being from the divine world. He was the beloved creation of the Akbar (the Most Great) charged to love Him. This is how his journey started in this world.

This wonderful world which is the 'matrix' of the human soul, serves two purposes altogether. Every atom of this universe, if seen from a divine perspective, reveals numerous beauties of that Unseen Beloved and spurs our soul to hasten to meet Him and, simultaneously, this same world, if viewed from our mortal eyes, becomes a fascinating forest of fabulous femes and fairies fettering our feet from following that 'Celestial Cherub' of changeless charm. Our choice has to be clear either to behold this mortal charm from an 'eternal' vista or witness this eternal magic of life from a 'mortal' vista. To wander and be lost in this forest ... or drink its fresh-gushing water, partake of its yummy fruits, and fresh and rejuvenated, rush to the Beloved waiting for us. The 'choice' we will be making will write our 'destiny' instantly, and that destiny will decide the further orientation of choice. With this sequential fluttering of the wings of 'free will' and 'destiny' the swan of the soul will soar to the sky.

Each choice we make, decides the progress or regress of our soul, exactly as in the game of 'Snake and Ladder'. Whatever uplifts our soul to the divine realm becomes a ladder for us and whatever tempts for our soul's degradation to this transient world becomes the snake. We have to win this game by perfecting our 'Karma' no matter how many births we have to pass by. It is impossible to believe that human soul was sent in this world in a haphazard process, without any basis or reason, for the first time, in such unjustified stations that one is too high and the other is too low, and that all this tortuous journey of a soul will fade into nothingness after a physical death. We see that the universe we are living in is working in an evolutionary manner, in a purposeful design, in a timeless and spaceless paradigm. It is logical to believe that every soul will continue its journey till it has completely learned how to respond to the spiritual challenges imposed upon it.

**Confidence and Satisfaction**

Life did not start suddenly out of a sexual act nor will it end abruptly with death. This belief in eternal life is a more soothing philosophy for mankind and fills us with everlasting hopes. Many people, like Henry Ford, strongly felt that believing in reincarnation is a hopeful sign for each individual that life is '**no longer a slave to the hands of the clock, and time is no longer limited**.' This belief in past life and life after death tells us that even if all our good works could not be rewarded here, rewards are waiting in the next lives ... such lives which have 'bodies' and 'feelings', expressions and satisfactions. Or else what is the use of 'reward'? It whispers to us that those who came and stabbed our heart will not go unpunished, even if they are spared in this world. Believing in past lives sets our soul in a state of complacence and forgiveness as we acknowledge our '*Karma*' and know that every affliction we suffered was our self-wrought destiny and nobody is to be blamed. With this realisation of our own responsibility, we become 'master of our fate and captain of our soul' and know that my deliverance is in my own hands and not depending on the mercy of the other.

> *He must unshackle himself by his own efforts, and must not degrade himself. He is his friend by himself, and by himself his own enemy.*
>
> (The Geetā, 6 : 5)

*Uddharet ātman ātmānam na ātmānam avasādayet;*
*Ātmiva hya ātmano sandhuh ātmaiva ripuh ātmanah.*

**Forgiveness and Liberation**

This belief that we all human beings are brethren floating in this eternal ocean of existence fills us with a compassion for all souls, for each person, because we acknowledge that each soul is in its journey, some coming behind, some gone forward but all started from the same 'Point' and all will immerse in the same 'Source'. This compassion melts all of us vainglories of riches and intellectual superiority and makes us humble and kind individuals. It arouses divine love in our hearts and a deep-felt empathy for those who are living in degraded states of their soul. Those who are sinners and engaged in heinous acts become objects of our mercy and not anger or revenge. Each one of us becomes a Christ and laments seeing their condition that ah, "**they know not what they do**".

Believing that life will not end here, infuses an untiring energy into our soul and we know for sure that our efforts made in this world are not lost, experiences achieved in one life will not be futile in the next, rather they will become a basis of our further progress in the realms hereafter. The dreams that we could not materialise, the missions we could not fulfil, the love we could not express, the places we could not visit, the people we could not meet, the hearts we could not explore, the errors we could not rectify, the burdens of soul we could not unload, the knowledge we could not share, the arts we could not learn, the skills we could not fully apply for the benefit of this world, the songs we could not sing into our friend's heart, the hopes of our parents we could not fulfil, the tears we could not wipe and the dimples of smiles we could not kiss, nothing is lost. We will find them, there, in that world where there is more freedom, more life and more permissions.

> Sorrow not if, in these days and on this earthly plane, things contrary to your wishes have been ordained and manifested by God, for days of blissful joy, of heavenly delight, are assuredly in

store for you. Worlds, holy and spiritually glorious, will be unveiled to your eyes. You are destined by Him, in this world and hereafter, to partake of their benefits, to share in their joys, and to obtain a portion of their sustaining grace. To each and everyone of them you will, no doubt, attain.

(Baha'u'llah)

* *

# More shades of Hinduism

Rs. 150/- pp: 232

HINDUISM
Clarified & Simplified

Rs. 249/- pp: 268
(HB)

Rs. 195/- pp: 268

Rs. 120/- pp: 152

Rs. 96/- pp: 168

Rs. 150/- pp: 268

Rs. 95/- pp: 163

Rs. 175/- pp: 296

Rs. 160/- pp: 342

Rs. 96/- pp: 119

Rs. 150/- pp: 152

Rs. 160/- pp: 201

Rs. 350/- pp: 308
(HB)

Rs. 80/- pp: 133

Rs. 60/- pp: 79

Rs. 195/- pp: 207
(HB)

Rs. 96/- pp: 190

Rs. 295/- pp: 306
(HB)

Rs. 150/- pp: 168

*Postage Rs. 25/- per book. Rs. 10/- extra for each additional book*

Available at all leading bookstores or log on to our online bookstore www.pustakmahal.com